LIVING *in* LOVE
with JESUS

Clothed in the Colors of His Love

DEE BRESTIN
KATHY TROCCOLI

NELSON IMPACT
A Division of Thomas Nelson Publishers
Since 1798

www.thomasnelson.com

FROM DEE:

To my youngest daughter, Annie

What a transformation has taken place in you—from a five-year-old orphan filled with fear to a beautiful young woman filled with faith, loving others with the mercy of the Father. I see in you, my darling, the colors of His love.

FROM DEE AND KATHY:

To all the women who are being transformed into glorious brides

Listen, O daughter, consider and give ear. . . .
The king is enthralled by your beauty;
*   honor him, for he is your lord. . . .*
All glorious is the princess within her chamber;
*   her gown is interwoven with gold.*
In embroidered garments she is led to the king. (Psalm 45:10–14a)

CONTENTS

Materials for *Living in Love with Jesus*

The workbook you are holding is an in-depth Bible study. It contains ten lessons, each divided into five days. Plan to spend at least thirty minutes each day alone with Jesus. We have also included Leader's Helps (Appendix A) in the back of each workbook.

What Do I Need for This Study?

All you *must* have for the study is this workbook and a Bible. However, the videos augment the study enormously. (Look for sales on various Web sites below. Divide up the cost between group members, or borrow the video from a church or someone who has already done the study.) On these thirty-minute videos, Dee and Kathy *both* teach. "Two are better than one," Solomon says, and the dynamic between these two very different Bible teachers will keep you listening, laughing, and learning. The book that accompanies this curriculum is supplementary and therefore helpful, but not essential. You do not need to complete the first study, *Falling in Love with Jesus*, before you begin this study.

Where Can I Purchase Materials?

Your local Christian bookstore or any of the following Web sites:

www.deebrestin.com
www.troccoli.com
www.thomasnelson.com
www.christianbook.com

If I Am Studying with a Small Group, Should I Do My First Lesson Ahead of Time?

Definitely. If, however, your group cannot pass out the workbooks until the first meeting, then watch the video, get acquainted, and begin the first lesson together. Then complete it at home and finish discussing it the second week. After that, always do the lesson ahead of time. Read with a pen or a highlighter, marking the text in the workbook that you want to keep in your heart.

Appendix B: Songs

We encourage you to turn here in your time alone with God and sing to Him or meditate on the words. Not only will this stir your heart to love Him more, it will bring great joy to your Lord. He delights in your praise.

APPENDIX C: MOVIE NIGHT

Have a girls' night out midway through the study. Watch Trimark's *Esther.* Discussion questions are provided here. (If you cannot rent it from your local Christian bookstore, dee-brestin.com and christianbook.com have it available for purchase.)

APPENDIX D: RESOURCES

Appendix D offers a listing of supplementary study resources on I John and Esther, as well as important Web sites (including Dee's and Kathy's) and referral information. In addition, a list of ministries approved by the Evangelical Council for Financial Accountability is provided as a recommendation for your financial giving.

MEMORY PASSAGES

The power to change our lives lies in the Word of God. Keep your heart open to memorizing Scripture. Tear out the perforated memory verse for the week and place it on the visor of your car or on your mirror. In this study you have a choice of Tracks. Track A helps you memorize key verses from the study. Track B helps you memorize one consecutive passage from 1 John.

Week 1: A Glorious Bride: Embroidered with Gold

The royal daughter is all glorious within the palace;
Her clothing is woven with gold.
She shall be brought to the King in robes of many colors.
(PSALM 45:13–14A NKJV)

A Glorious Bride: Embroidered with Gold

We have been overwhelmed by the response to our first curriculum, *Falling in Love with Jesus*. So many of you, from eighteen to eighty, have written and told us how understanding that Jesus is your Bridegroom has brought your relationship with Him to a whole new level. Wherever you are in your singleness or marriage, you know you have a perfect Bridegroom. You feel cherished, and you are experiencing a deeper intimacy with Him.

What an exciting journey this has been for us as well. We'd like to tell you about just one amazing weekend when we were invited to minister at a two-day event. *Falling in Love with Jesus* was the theme, and it was being held at an elegant hotel in Atlanta. At this event the committee had planned all the pomp and circumstance involved with a royal wedding reception in order to bless four hundred women who were in full-time ministry. We watched as these women completely absorbed the pampering, the attention, and the reminder that they are loved as the Bride of Christ. Facials, manicures, and massages were available, without cost, before the start of the event. White flowers, fine china gleaming in candlelight, and displays of wedding gowns were arranged throughout the hotel. In the evening, when the women returned to their rooms, they found rose petals and chocolates scattered across their bedspreads. It was all magnificent.

Several humorous things happened that weekend, which we later realized made a perfect parallel for *this* study, *Living in Love with Jesus*.

(Dee) My plane arrived first. I waited with the retreat coordinator, Mary Francis, outside the security area. Darlene, a Delta flight attendant on the committee, went right to the gate to greet Kathy when she got off the plane. Darlene watched as each woman walked through the door. When the last passenger walked off and they closed the door, she was dismayed. No Kathy! She hurriedly called Mary Francis on her cell phone. I could hear Darlene's voice, filled with panic:

"Kathy wasn't on the plane!"

I thought for a moment and then realized what had happened. Smiling, I said, "Mary Francis, Kathy *was* on the plane. Trust me. Darlene just didn't recognize her. People always look for the 'album cover Kathy.' You know—the hair done, the makeup, the gorgeous clothes. Don't worry. I'll watch for her. She'll be coming up the escalator any minute."

Sure enough, a few minutes later, Kathy appeared, easily lost in the crowd in her typical ball cap, jeans, cowboy boots, and leather jacket. I waved to get her attention. She smiled that recognizable smile, and the committee all breathed a sigh of relief.

The situation became more humorous when we arrived at the hotel. Our van pulled up to a side entrance, which was lined with urns overflowing with flowers.

(Kathy) I was walking in to greet the women when I was stopped.

"Wait, wait, wait! You can't come in yet."

Dee and I began to see what was so sweetly planned. The women started to unroll a white lace runner. A bubble machine was turned on over the door, and bubbles began to fill the air. When I saw what they were doing, I lightheartedly pushed Dee aside, saying:

"You've done this before. Get out of the way! This may be my only chance!"

This was a moment I didn't want to rush. I began to walk with an exaggerated "bride step," singing, "Here Comes the Bride." Everyone laughed hysterically. Part of the comedy was that instead of wearing a delicate white wedding gown and demure veil, I marched in wearing my traveling clothes: jeans, leather jacket, and ball cap. I had on no makeup, and to be quite honest, I had to catch a really early flight, so I had not even showered. I was surely not a typical bride!

PHOTO OF KATHY'S ENTRANCE
(Courtesy of Susan Stewart)

It hit us later that this picture was a quite accurate portrayal of us as His betrothed. . . .

This week we are going to look at some of the pictures our Lord gives in Scripture of brides—some caught off guard, some gloriously adorned. For a great wedding day is coming, and our Bridegroom, Jesus, is coming for us. We want to be prepared.

Do your homework *before* you gather in your groups. In your groups you will be watching a video that will correspond with the lesson for that week. You will see a page for video notes. If you learn better simply by listening, you needn't fill it out. But many women find filling in the blanks helps them remember key points. There are also spaces for you to jot down anything you want to remember.

We challenge you to give your daily time with God top priority and attention. You will discover that much of the emphasis of 1 John is on the difference between the real and the counterfeit. It is so easy to walk like a Christian, talk like a Christian, and even be a Christian, yet have so much of the counterfeit in us. One of the key ways to drive the counterfeit from our lives is to pour truth into our souls. Determine now to be faithful, giving your time with Jesus priority, and with a heart open to His Spirit. Read with a pen or a highlighter, marking things in the workbook text that you want to keep in your heart. Our Bridegroom longs for faithful brides.

You will also find a memory passage for this week on a perforated page at the back of the book. Begin learning it right away so you can review it each day. Set a high standard for yourself and you not only will be taken to new spiritual heights, but you will help your sisters in this group to grow as well.

One key to living in love with Jesus is pouring truth into your soul, so set your heart to do that from the beginning.

One key to living in love with Jesus is pouring truth into your soul, so set your heart to do that from the beginning.

VIDEO NOTES FOR WEEK 1
A GLORIOUS BRIDE: EMBROIDERED WITH GOLD
Thoughts I want to remember:

_____

_____

_____

_____

_____

_____

_____

1. What did the woman cleaning the hotel rooms ask Kathy?
   You ain't the same woman?
   we will be transformed into a bride

2. John's Gospel helps us _fall_ in love with Jesus. He wrote the Gospel so that "you may believe that Jesus is the Christ, the Son of God, and that by believing you may have _____ in his name" (John 20:31).

3. John's first letter was written later, to revive that life, to help us _live_ in love with Jesus. He tells us: "And now, dear children, continue in him, so that when he appears we may be _____ and _____ before him at his coming" (1 John 2:28).

4. In the parable of the wedding banquet in Matthew 22, the king asked one guest: *"How did you get in here without _wedding clothes_?"* The man was speechless.

we are like the one who gave us birth
God gave me birth.

Then the king told the attendants, "Tie him hand and foot, and throw him outside, into the darkness, where there will be _____ and *gnashing of teeth* " (Matthew 22:12–13). In this passage, the wedding garment seems to represent *Salvation* .

faith/good works

5. In the description of the "Wedding of the Lamb," we are told that "fine linen stands for the _____ _____ _____ _____ _____" (Revelation 19:8b). In this passage, the wedding garment seems to represent *the holy life* .

6. James tells us "Faith by itself, if it is not accompanied by action, is *dead* " (James 2:17).

bring back to life

7. Define "revived." *brought back from the dead*

8. "The colors of His love" is a phrase we hope will ignite your *imagination* on what is possible as you live in love with Jesus.

Live in light. Die to self. Speak truth. Plan good. Be merciful

9. In Scripture, the color *gold* represents the finest and the best.

10. Job said, "When he has tested me, I will come forth as *gold* " (Job 23:10).

God will make us complete

11. Psalm 45 begins with "My heart is stirred by a noble theme." What is this noble theme? *Jesus is coming back for his bride.*

12. A scepter of *justice* will be the scepter of your kingdom.

13. All glorious am I, *the princess* , within my chamber. My gown is interwoven with *gold* . (The character of God is interwoven throughout my character.) In embroidered garments I am led to the *king* .

colors of His love

GETTING ACQUAINTED

1. Going around the circle, be ready to share your name and a response to *one* of the following: A time when you were caught unprepared that was funny or stressful.

_____

What you are looking forward to in this group.

_____

2. What stood out most to you in the video? Why?

_____

3. Some groups *particularly* spur you on to a deeper walk with Jesus. They are blessed because they are made up of women of depth who hunger for more of Jesus. How can you, as an individual, prepare and share so as to make this group the best it can be?

BECOMING HIS BETROTHED

God gives us many pictures in Scripture to show us He wants intimacy with us: He tells us we are His children, that we are His body, but also, that we are His Bride. God the Son is the Bridegroom, and the church, or the true body of believers, is His Bride.

How interesting it is to examine some of the wedding customs in the days Jesus was on earth, and to see how they make a beautiful parallel to our ultimate Bridegroom.

The Jewish wedding ceremony in the days of Jesus took place in three parts. Each part was symbolic. Before the first part, or the betrothal, could occur, a "bride price" had to be paid. This involved intense bargaining between the father of the bride and the father of the groom. The bride price was very steep. The price was comparable to what you might pay for a new house today.

1. According to 1 Peter 1:18–19, what "bride price" was paid for you?

   the blood of christ

2. The "bride price" has been paid, but you must receive it through faith. When the Holy Spirit helps you to fully understand your sin, your depravity, your heart will cry out to a Holy God to be rescued. He has provided a way for you to be cleansed, to put on "a garment of righteousness," so that you will not be ashamed. Meditate carefully on Romans 10:9–11 and write down everything you discover.

   believe in your heart that Jesus is Lord. Confess it with your heart and mouth.

It is vital to see that it is not enough to confess Jesus as Lord with your mouth. There are many who profess, but one day, because nothing happened in their hearts, Jesus will say, "I never knew you." The heart of *Living in Love with Jesus* is the first letter of John. John continually differentiates between the counterfeit and the genuine. When salvation is genuine, there has been a heart change, and out of that heart will flow a change in behavior that lasts.

(Kathy) I remember when I had the veil completely lifted from my eyes, when I first grasped what Jesus did for me on the cross. Crucifixes were so much a part of my environment growing up. My family had them hanging over the headboards in most of the bedrooms. Some were

even on the tops of dressers with candles around them. As a child I rarely saw adults without a crucifix around their necks. It wasn't just the cross, it was the full body of Jesus in agony.

Even at church, when I'd focus on the huge crucifix above the altar I was numb to the sight of it all. I had seen it so often: the crown of thorns, the blood trickling down His face, the bleeding wound in His side, the nails in His hands and feet. It all just seemed like some great tragedy from a Shakespearean play. I was removed from it because I didn't understand what it really had to do with *my* life. Yet a time came when I realized the significance of what Jesus did on the cross. I wept on and off for several months. My heart was pierced with the knowledge of Christ and what He had done for me. I would never be the same again. I understood the true meaning of His death, the great mystery of God's plan to reconcile me with Himself. The cross became sacred.

3. If your heart "has been pierced" as Kathy's was, do you remember how you felt when you first understood your sinfulness and what Jesus did for you on the cross? If so, share something about it and how you responded.

When Pastor Mike called for people who wanted
to receive Christ

Jesus told the parable of the ten virgins. All thought they were ready for their bridegroom's return, but five were not. Read the story carefully in Matthew 25:1–13. It is important to remember, when interpreting a parable, not to focus too intensely on individual elements, but on the main point, or you *will* miss the forest for the trees! In writing about those who have tried to give a particular meaning to the lamps, the vessels, and the oil in this parable, John Calvin writes: "We ought not to trouble ourselves much with minute investigations, which have nothing to do with what Christ intended."[1]

4. A. With this in mind, as you read Matthew 25:1–13, simply describe what happened. Don't try to interpret yet—hurried interpretations are often wrong. Wait, for the other Scriptures will give you additional light.

The wise virgins had oil, while the foolish
virgins were out getting oil, the bridegroom
arrived.

B. What observations do you have of the painting on page 8, *The Foolish Virgins?*

The virgins are searching frantically
for oil

5. In the story just preceding the parable of the virgins, there is another story of foolish and wise people. What other adjective is used to describe the wise servant? (See Matthew 24:45.) _faithful_

6. In the parable of the virgins, the wise and the foolish are separated by an event (the return of the bridegroom). Likewise, in Matthew 7:24–27, the wise and the foolish are separated by an event (a storm). In the story involving the storm, how did the wise and the foolish look the same? Yet what was different about them?

Had same instructions — wise built on rock, foolish on sand

7. How could you tell that the foolish people in the above stories were counterfeit believers?

THE FOOLISH VIRGINS
J. JAMES TISSOT (1895 -1899)

8. What do you think is the primary point of the parable of the ten virgins?

to be always ready

Begin memorizing your memory passage. (See the perforated sheet at the back of the workbook.)

If you have asked Jesus to forgive you, if you have given yourself to Him as your Lord with your whole heart, then you are His betrothed. Wherever you are in your singleness or your marriage, you have a perfect Bridegroom who will never leave you nor forsake you. He will never be unfaithful to you. There is a ring on your finger. Your Bridegroom delights in your praise. In the privacy of your home, spend some time singing love songs from Appendix B in the back to Him.

I Am Going Away to Prepare
a Place for You

After the betrothal, in the days of Jesus, the bridegroom went away in order to add a room to his father's house for his bride. It usually took about a year, but the actual length of time the groom was gone varied.

9. One possible parallel is in John 14:1–3. What do you see?

   Jesus is going to prepare a room for me.

   Max Lucado writes in *When Christ Comes,*

   > *He is preparing a place. . . . He knows exactly what you need. You needn't worry about getting bored or tired or weary with seeing the same people or singing the same songs. . . . Trust the promises of Christ. "I have ample space for you; I have prepared a place for you."*

10. In the days of Jesus, it wasn't until the *father* said all was ready that the groom came back in a great processional with his friends, surprising the bride. Read Matthew 24:36–38. What do you learn in this passage about the return of Christ?

    only the Father knows when Christ will come.

11. When the father said all was ready, the groom would come with his friends, in a great processional. There is a beautiful picture of Solomon's wedding day in the Song of Songs that is a foreshadowing of a much greater and wondrous processional. Read it in the Song of Songs 3:6–11.

    A. Describe the grandeur of the processional. What stands out to you and why (Song of Songs 3:6–8)?

       Solomon made his own carriage

    B. What evidence can you find in this passage that the bridegroom delighted in his bride and in pleasing her?

       "Its interior lovingly inlaid

12. A. When the bridegroom came, one of his friends would blow a ram's horn, called a

shofar, and the bride would hear it and know her bridegroom was very near. What parallel do you see in Matthew 24:31?

a horn was also blown.

B. During the bridegroom's absence, the bride was preparing her wedding garment. Wedding gowns have been important throughout the ages, and in Scripture they are deeply symbolic. Your memory passage this week (if you are doing Track A) involves the wedding garment. See if you can write the verse here without looking at it:

C. It is fascinating to study the passages that involve the wedding garment. What does the wedding garment represent?

faith   our preparation for Christ

13. In Matthew 22:1–13, read the story of a king who gave a wedding for his son. Some historians say that at a royal wedding, not only was the bride attired, but fine linen, white and clean, was given to every guest who was invited. Describe what happened in verses 11–13. What does the wedding garment seem to represent in this passage? Why?

faithful,   respect & appropriately
pure, ready   attired

14. In Revelation 19:6–8, what are we told the wedding garment represents?

righteousness

Some would say that in Matthew the wedding garment represents faith, or salvation. Yet in Revelation, it seems to represent a holy life, or righteous acts. Which is it?

We are saved by faith, yet, as James says, "faith by itself, if it is not accompanied by action, is dead" (James 2:17). Another way of saying this is that faith without works makes no sense. Unless it is a deathbed conversion, you *should* be able to see a change in the person's life, and that change should continue. True faith will result in a life that reflects the Lord. John Calvin explains:

> As to the wedding-garment, is it faith, or is it a holy life? This is a useless controversy; for faith cannot be separated from good works, nor do good works proceed from any other source than from faith. But Christ intended only to state that the Lord calls us on the express condition of our being renewed by the Spirit after his image . . . we must put off the old man. . . .[3]

15. Our transformation begins at salvation, but as we "continue in Him," the transformation continues. As you look back over your life since you put your trust in Christ, name

some of the ways you have seen the Spirit of God make a change in you.

becoming sober.

Not trying to run the show myself.

Continue learning your memory passage.

WE AIN'T GOING TO BE THE SAME WOMAN

(Kathy) We've had a lot of laughs talking about our "wedding weekend" in Atlanta. I got razzed about how I walked down the aisle, and about my transformation from grunge to glamour. Neither Dee nor I knew it would be such a perfect analogy for this book.

The funny incidents just kept happening. Dee and I went up to our rooms to change. We passed the woman cleaning the rooms and visited with her a little bit.

Later, when I came out, I had changed from my ball cap and jeans to a lovely suit. I'd done my hair and my makeup. I passed the same woman Dee and I had talked to earlier, and though I said "Hi," she just stared at me, unresponsive. A few minutes later I heard a confused voice call down to me:

"S'cuse me. S'cuse me." She moved closer. "You ain't da same woman I saw before—are ya?"

I smiled at her inquisitiveness. I knew I looked different. "Yes, I certainly am."

When I told Dee, she laughed so hard. She said, "This is perfect, Kath. We can tell women that as they follow the principles in 1 John, a transformation will continue in them. Right now they may be a bride in a ball cap, but they can become radiant brides, brides who are confident and unashamed at His coming."

If you know Jesus, if you have put your trust in what He did for you on the cross, the process has begun. You are in the betrothal period. You are now getting ready for your Bridegroom's return. The true and eternal transformation will *not* happen with makeup, surgery, or wardrobe—it will happen because of His life being poured into you: more of His light, more of His truth, more of His mercy. This is the only way it will happen. As His bride, we can be bought and transformed by no other means.

Our Bridegroom has gone away, but He will be back.

16. In 1 John 3:2–3, how does John explain that this time of separation is also the time of preparation?

No one can see the kingdom of God unless he is born again.

Purify yourself

This is a topical study, which differs from a book study in that you look at a particular topic rather than going verse by verse through a book. The core of this study, *Living in Love with Jesus,* consists of four principles found in 1 John that will help us be transformed into beautiful brides:

- ∽ Clothed in light
- ∽ Clothed in death
- ∽ Clothed in truth
- ∽ Clothed in mercy

All of the above are characteristics of the Lord. As we are being transformed into His image, they should also be true of us.

Review your memory passage.

17. What do you discover about the Lord from the following passages? From the above list, find the characteristic of the Lord and anything you discover about it. (They are not in the same order as above!)

A. 1 John 1:5 ___God is light; In him there is no darkness___

B. 1 John 2:20–21 ___truth___

C. 1 John 3:16 ___Love; lay down your life; death___

D. 1 John 4:7–8 ___God is Love___

Day 4

THOU ART THE FAIREST OF MEN

The first part of this wedding psalm, Psalm 45, describes the amazing Bridegroom, and the second part, His Bride. William Binnie, D.D., writes: "When a prince sets his affections on a woman of lowly rank, and takes her home to be his wife, the two are so united that her debts become his, his wealth and honours become hers."[4]

18. Sometimes we write from our heads, sometimes from our hearts. What does the psalmist say here in verse 1?

___My heart is stirred by a noble theme___

Read the following translations of Psalm 45:2a:

> *You are the most excellent of men.* (NIV)
> *Thou art fairer than the children of men.* (KJV)
> *You are the fairest of all.* (TLB)

One suggestion would be to sing "Fairest Lord Jesus" to your Bridegroom in your alone time. Sing it with all your heart and soul and mind. Charles Spurgeon noted that as the psalmist began to pour out his affections to the Lord, the Lord revealed Himself to him. Begin your time alone with the Lord today by pouring out your affection to Him.

> *Fairest Lord Jesus, ruler of all nature,*
> *O Thou of God and man the Son, Thee will I cherish,*
> *Thee will I honor, Thou, my soul's glory, joy, and crown!*
> *Fair are the meadows, fairer still the woodlands,*
> *Robed in the blooming garb of spring: Jesus is fairer,*
> *Jesus is purer, who makes the woeful heart to sing.*
> *Fair is the sunshine, fairer still the moonlight,*
> *And all the twinkling starry host: Jesus shines brighter,*
> *Jesus shines purer, than all the angels heaven can boast.*
> *Beautiful Savior! Lord of all nations!*
> *Son of God and Son of Man! Glory and honor,*
> *Praise, adoration, now and forevermore be thine!* (Public Domain)

19. What do you cherish in Jesus as your Bridegroom? List a few specific ways He has been a husband to you in protection, provision, and faithfulness.

    Love, purity, power, faithfulness, redeemer.

In the Song of Songs, the Shulamite maiden praised her bridegroom, who was a foreshadowing of Christ:

> *My lover is radiant and ruddy,*
> > *outstanding among ten thousand.*
> *His head is purest gold . . .*
> (Song of Songs 5:10–11a)

20. Read the vision John had of the Bridegroom:

> *I saw heaven standing open and there before me was a white horse, whose rider is called* <u>*Faithful and True*</u>. *With justice he judges and makes war. His eyes are like blazing fire, and on his head are many crowns. He has a name written on him that no one knows but he himself. He is dressed in a robe dipped in blood, and his name is the Word of God. The armies of heaven were following him, riding on white horses and dressed in fine linen, white and clean. Out of his mouth comes a sharp sword with which to strike down the nations. "He will rule them with an iron scepter." He treads the winepress of the fury of the wrath of God Almighty. On his robe and on his thigh he has this name written:*
>
> KING OF KINGS AND LORD OF LORDS. (Revelation 19:11–16)

Now read the vision of the Bridegroom in Psalm 45:3–7. What similarities do you see?

ride forth victoriously
a scepter of justice

21. What does it mean to you, in the difficulties or challenges of your life right now, that you have a Bridegroom who is just, faithful, and true—and who will fight for you? Be specific.

One suggestion is to sing the first and third verses of Julia Ward Howe's "Battle Hymn of the Republic" in your individual quiet time as a prayer from your heart.

> *Mine eyes have seen the glory of the coming of the Lord;*
> *He is trampling out the vintage where the grapes of wrath are stored;*
> *He hath loosed the fateful lightning of His terrible swift sword;*
> *His truth is marching on.*
>
> *Glory! Glory! Hallelujah! Glory! Glory! Hallelujah! Glory! Glory! Hallelujah!*
> *His truth is marching on.*
>
> *He has sounded forth the trumpet that shall never sound retreat;*
> *He is sifting out the hearts of men before His judgment seat.*
> *Oh, be swift, my soul, to answer Him; be jubilant, my feet;*
> *Our God is marching on.*
>
> *Glory! Glory! Hallelujah! Glory! Glory! Hallelujah! Glory! Glory! Hallelujah!*
> *Our God is marching on.*
> (Public Domain)

22. What else do you learn about our Bridegroom from Psalm 45:7–9?

Daughters of kings, the royal bride in gold

(Kathy) I loved to read passages like the above to my mother in her last weeks and days on earth. I said, "Mom, Jesus is preparing a place for you . . . isn't that comforting?" I knew it had to comfort her soul.

A GLORIOUS BRIDEGROOM
AND A BEAUTIFUL BRIDE

The subtitle of this study is "Clothed in the Colors of His Love," a phrase that we hope will ignite your imagination. Our God is so lavish in the ways He loves that we cannot name the colors of His love any more than we can list the colors in the feathers of the peacock, the petals of the wildflowers, or the leaves of autumn.

23. As you look at the world God created, what are some of your favorite colors?

_____ red, blue, purple, green, orange _____

24. Meditate on Psalm 19:1–6.
    A. What does the splendor of the heavens declare?

    _____ the glory of God _____

    B. Why is it that every single individual, even in the most remote area of the earth, is accountable to realize there is a God?

       Psalm 19:4 is quoted in Romans 10:18 when Paul is making a case that shows that everyone has "heard" about God, because of creation.

    C. To what does the psalmist compare the sun that faithfully rises each morning, flooding the earth with light

    _____ the bridegroom coming _____

Jonathan Edwards writes:

> *Therein the Sun of Righteousness rises from under the earth, as the sun appears to do in the morning, and comes forth as a bridegroom. He rose as the joyful, glorious bridegroom of his church; for Christ, especially as risen again, is the proper bridegroom or husband, of his church . . .*[5]

Although we have told you we cannot name the colors of His love because there are so many, we can tell you that in Scripture, gold often represents the finest and the best.

Can you say your memory verse without looking at it?

We've paraphrased the following from Psalm 45. Insert your name:

All glorious am I, _____ Lynne _____, within my chamber. My gown is interwoven with _gold_. (The character of God is interwoven throughout my character.) In embroidered garments I am led to the King.

We've often talked about what suffering and "picking up one's cross" produce in the heart of a woman. The fires of life will refine and purify your character into a magnificent gold if you allow God to use them as He desires. Many of us know women who already "glisten" with the attributes of God.

25. What does gold represent in the following passages? *faith*

faithful

    A. Job 23:10 *when he has tested me I come forth as gold*

    B. 1 Peter 1:7 *your faith of greater worth than gold*

It has been said that a refiner of gold, the craftsman who burns the impurities out of gold over the fire, knows that the gold is genuine and pure when he can see his face in it. In the same way, Jesus knows we are genuine and pure when He can see His reflection in us.

26. With the above verses in mind, how might you become a glorious bride, with a gown interwoven with gold?

    Be like Christ pure, loving, kind, patient, faithful

27. Meditate on the description of the bride in Psalm 45:10–15.

    A. What do you think verse 10 means?

    forget your past

In the story of Lot's wife, she looked back, not willing to be truly severed from her past. In contrast, Ruth left her people and her father's house to follow God. Jesus asks us to "forsake" all other loves, to let go of the things we thought were important before coming to know Him, and to love Him first and best. This "dying" to what the world holds dear is key to transforming us into a beautiful bride. (We'll look at this in depth in Weeks 6 and 7.)

    B. How does the Lord feel about such a bride, according to verse 11?

    enthralled

    C. Describe the princess, according to verse 13.

    glorious, gown interwoven with gold

Within her secret chambers her glory is great. Though unseen of men her Lord sees her, and commends her. "It doth not yet appear what we shall be." [1 John 3:2b KJV] Or the passage may be understood as meaning within herself—her beauty is not outward only or mainly; the choicest of her charms are to be found in her heart, her secret character, her inward desires.[6]

(Charles Spurgeon)

D. Describe the mood, according to verse 15, of that great wedding day.

joy + gladness

> *. . . Have you ever noticed the way a groom looks at his bride during the wedding? . . . Most miss it. Most miss it because they are looking at her. But when other eyes are on the bride, I sneak a peek at the groom. If the light is just so and the angle just right, I can see a tiny reflection in his eyes. Her reflection. And the sight of her reminds him why he is here. His jaw relaxes and his forced smile softens. He forgets he's wearing a tux. He forgets his sweat-soaked shirt. When he sees her, any thought of escape becomes a joke again. For it's written all over his face, "Who could bear to live without this bride?"*[7]

(Max Lucado)

28. What do you think you will remember from this week's study? How will you apply it to your life?

Be a pure + faithful bride + loving . Glorify the Lord.

PRAYER TIME

Close in silent prayer today, asking each woman to pray silently for the woman on her right, that she would see significant changes in her life as a result of this study. Pray she would be a faithful bride, spending time with the Lord, and that she would be transformed. After a few minutes, the discussion leader might lead in this closing song:

> *In my life, Lord, be glorified, be glorified*
> *In my life, Lord, be glorified today.*
> *In your Bride, Lord, be glorified, be glorified*
> *In your Bride, Lord, be glorified today.*

Words and Music by Bob Kilpatrick, © 1978 Bob Kilpatrick Music; P.O. Box 2383, Fair Oaks, CA 95628. All Rights Reserved. International Copyright Secured. Used by Permission.

OVERVIEW OF 1 JOHN:

Week 2: WHAT IS SHE WEARING?
Week 3: BLACK AND WHITE

*The life of a man who professes to be living in
God must bear the stamp of Christ.*
(1 JOHN 2:6 PHILLIPS)

WHAT IS SHE WEARING?

(Kathy)

I tell a story in my book *My Life Is in Your Hands* of a flight attendant I could not help but notice because of her undeniable radiance. Midway through the flight I got up and walked back to use the rest room. She was seated at the back of the plane, and I even surprised myself when I asked her: "You love Jesus, don't you?"

She looked up at me, and with a glow in her eyes, she said, "Yes. How did you know?"

I told her that I had watched her, and her actions and her countenance spoke loudly to me about her love for Him.

The river of life inside that flight attendant splashed onto everyone around her. And if she had never spoken a word that day, all those coming in contact with her would have seen clearly the God of the universe living inside her heart.[1]

When people meet us, do they recognize Jesus in us?

What is she wearing?

The answer must be Jesus.

(Dee) This week we are beginning our overview of 1 John. The main message of this letter is that if we know Jesus, then His life must be evident in us. If He is the heart of us, it should be evident in our countenance, our actions, and our choices. When Kathy sings "The Heart of Me," this is the message of 1 John. If Jesus truly lives within us, then we will feel what He feels, see what He sees, love as He loves. His love, His life, will flow from us to others.

This life begins when we put our trust in Christ, for it is then that His Spirit is born within us. We cannot be beautiful in and of ourselves. It is only Christ that makes us beautiful. But the exciting part is that this supernatural life of the Lord can be nurtured until it overflows to others. People will be drawn to us and will even ask questions about the hope within us. That is when we can tell them honestly that the difference in us is Jesus.

VIDEO NOTES FOR WEEK 2
WHAT IS SHE WEARING?

Thoughts I want to remember:

_____

_____

1. *The life of a man who professes to be living in God must bear the* ___Stamp___ *of* ___Christ___. (1 John 2:6 PHILLIPS)

2. In the story of the Good Samaritan, Jesus says the Samaritan was doing a better job of bearing the ___mark___ of a believer.

3. Francis Schaeffer said, "The world cares nothing for doctrine; the world is watching to see how we ___Love___."

4. Jesus said:

   A new command I give you: ___Love___ ___one___ ___another___. *As I have loved you, so you must love one another. By this all men will* ___know___ *that you are my disciples, if you love one another.* (John 13:34–35)

5. One way you can tell what is most important is by what is said when ___time___ is running out.

6. When you look at the life of Jesus, what you see is ___Love___.

7. At the last supper, when time was running out, Jesus said:

   My children, I will be with you only a little ___longer___. (John 13:33a)

   As I have ___loved___ *you, so you must* ___love___ *one another.* (John 13:34b)

   By this all men will know that you are my ___disciples___, *if you* ___love___ ___one___ ___another___. (John 13:35)

ICEBREAKER *(Hear from several women for each question.)*

1. If you knew your death was imminent, as many people did on 9/11/2001, and you could call someone, whom would you call and what would you say?
   ___my children ← "I love you" → My friends___

2. What stood out most to you in the video? Why?
   ___Jesus love me & wants me to love him & all others___

Clothed in:
Light
Death to self
Truth
Mercy

Day 1

THE IMPRINT OF A CHRISTIAN

(Dee) I was showing my grandchildren how to make an imprint of a leaf. I gave them each an autumn-colored crayon and a leaf from a backyard tree. Seven-year-old Emily, the eldest, led the way. She placed an oak leaf under a piece of white paper and rubbed the long side of an unwrapped Indian red crayon over the top. The more she rubbed, the more an elongated oak leaf emerged. She grinned, showing the space where her two front teeth had been, and proudly held up her creation for her siblings to admire.

Five-year-old Jessa earnestly rubbed a harvest gold crayon over an elm leaf. "Gramma, look!" She gave a little cry of delight as the imprint appeared: the stem, the veins, the tiny teeth all around the edge—a distinct and perfectly compact elm leaf.

Three-year-old Simeon hopped up on the chair, insisting: "I can do it!" With a little help and encouragement to be gentle, he rubbed a blazing crimson crayon over a maple leaf. He beamed as it emerged. "I did it! I did it!" And he had. There it was—that most familiar of leaves, the maple, aflame in autumn brilliance.

There was no mistaking an oak for an elm, or an elm for a maple. Each had its own distinct imprint.

> *But what is the imprint of a Christian?*

When people brush up against us, whether it is a quick brush or a more intense one, can they tell who gave us birth? Do they recognize the hands, the heart, the love of Jesus? The heart of 1 John can be found in this verse:

> *The life of a man who professes to be living in God must bear the stamp of Christ.* (1 John 2:6 PHILLIPS)

If the image of Christ has faded in you from the time when you first knew Him, John's letter will tell you how to revive His life in you. This study is a topical study of the letter of John. We will look at four characteristics of the Lord that, as we apply them to our lives, will make His stamp clear in us.

> Because He is light, we must walk in the light.
> Because He laid down His life, we must lay down our lives.
> Because He is truth, we must live by the truth.
> Because He is mercy, we must be merciful.

Remember the story of the ten virgins? They all seemed to be ready for Jesus—but five were genuine, and five were counterfeit.

1. Today, read through the five short chapters of 1 John (near the very end of your Bible) to gain familiarity with the themes. Simply note, as you read, the many times John makes a differentiation between the genuine believer and the counterfeit believer. Some phrases to watch for are:

> *If we claim . . .*
> *If we say . . .*
> *Anyone who . . .*
> *Everyone who . . .*
> *Who is the liar?*

Then come back to this page and list just a few of the characteristics that differentiate the genuine believer from the counterfeit along with the corresponding reference. (Sometimes John only shows one side, and you will need to imagine the opposite.) We will be looking at this more closely in the coming weeks, but for now, see if you can discover just a few of the differences between the counterfeit and the genuine.

COUNTERFEIT	GENUINE
1:6 Claims to have fellowship with God yet walks in darkness	1:7 Walks in the light as he is in the light
_____	_____
_____	_____
_____	_____
_____	_____

(Kathy) When I first read through 1 John, I thought, **What?!** *I fail every day! Is John saying I am damned?* If you are having those feelings, hang on, because next week you will gain insight into John's "black and white" statements. You will see that they actually can *increase* your confidence rather than making you want to run for the hills.

Begin learning this week's memory passage.

Day 2

COUNTERFEIT CLOTHES

So often we make the mark of a true believer something quite different from what Jesus does. The Pharisees thought it consisted of appearances and adhering to certain rituals. They were very critical of Jesus because He lived differently from the way they did. He healed on the

Sabbath, He ate with sinners, and He treated women, even those with a shameful past, with respect. Most biting of all, Jesus called *them* hypocrites. In an attempt to trap and expose Jesus, the Pharisees and the Sadducees questioned Him. It is interesting that their questions began right after Jesus told the story of a man who came to the wedding banquet not wearing a wedding garment. Jesus had skillfully answered several of their questions when an expert of the law came up with the most important question.

2. Read Matthew 22:34–40.

    A. What question did the expert in the law ask and why?

    _____

    B. How did Jesus answer? What do you think He meant by verse 40?

    _____

    _____

    _____

3. In Matthew 23, Jesus exposes the teachers of the law and the Pharisees. What does He say in each of the following passages?

    A. Matthew 23:4_____

    _____

    B. Matthew 23:5_____

    _____

    C. Matthew 23:23_____

    _____

    D. Matthew 23:25–26 _____

    _____

4. Luke also describes this interaction between Jesus and the Pharisees and includes the story of the good Samaritan. Read Luke 10:25–37 and study the painting on page 26 by Jacopo Bassano. Note the Levite in the background—his posture and hurried gait. Note the determination and effort of the Samaritan.

    A. Why, according to Luke 10:29, did the Pharisee ask, "Who is my neighbor?"

    _____

    _____

"THE GOOD SAMARITAN"
JACOPO BASSANO (1517/18–1592)

B. Who fell into the Pharisee's trap? Why?

_____

_____

It is important to realize that Jesus was not saying that the Samaritan was a believer, nor that the priest or the Levite who hurried past the wounded man were necessarily unbelievers, but that the Samaritan was doing a better job of bearing the mark of a Christian. He was bearing the image of Christ, for he was showing Christlike love. The Pharisees were making the mark of a believer something quite different from Jesus' example. How important it is to realize that we, even though we may know the Lord, are susceptible to the same trap.

The following story Kathy tells illustrates this so clearly, but we want to preface it by saying that this is not to be interpreted as bashing a particular belief, for that is the exact opposite of the message of this book. The Lord has given us a deep love and appreciation for the Church, the body of true believers, and for the unique dimensions that various denominations can bring to the body of Christ. But this story illustrates how sometimes even believers can fail to bear the stamp of Christ. We confuse the genuine imprint with a lot of other things, influenced by man's wisdom—by what our particular denomination or circle of friends emphasizes as important.

(Kathy) I was a new Christian when I was getting asked to sing at many different places on Long Island and in New York City. I was immediately thrown into a sea of churches: Assembly of God, Catholic, Baptist . . . I was often drowning in the confusion of all the different theologies I was hearing.

> _Speak in tongues._
> _Don't speak in tongues._
> _Be immersed._

Be sprinkled.
Raise your hands.
Don't raise your hands.
Sing quietly.
Sing loudly.
Don't sing at all.

I'd often come home from singing at church events or coffeehouses with a heavy heart. I found that the simple realization that Jesus loved me and wanted me to love others was suddenly clouded by what seemed like so many divisive ways of expressing Christianity. Arrogance permeated so many places. People thought their church "did it right." People thought their beliefs were "the true beliefs." People thought everyone else was "a little off base." It affected me deeply because in my idealism, I expected we would live together as one big happy family, being cherished by a big and holy God. I remember being saddened at the creeping feelings of disillusionment that were slowly smothering my newfound joy.

I came home late one night, after singing at yet another church service. I went into my bedroom and sat on the floor against the wall. I was weary, confused, and discouraged. Looking up to God I said,

Lord, I don't know what to make of all of this.
Is this the way Christians are?
Is this what I am going to be around?

I let out a big sigh and remained quiet for a while. My kite had been soaring so high and now it felt as if it were taking a nosedive. Since then I've learned it is in times like these, in the stillness, that Jesus comes gently. This is what I sensed He was saying to me that night:

Open the Gospels. Look at Me. Look at My life.
Take in the things I've said. I will teach you.

He is so wonderful like that. When we are at the end of *ourselves*, He comes to us and shows us *Himself*. Even now when moments of frustration arise, when there is obvious hypocrisy or twisting of the Word of God, I go back to that moment.

I continued to travel all over the New York area and had quickly become a national recording artist. At the time, I traveled by myself, with just my guitar and a little box of records to sell. I was constantly meeting new people: in hotels, on planes, at lunches and dinners. Conversations with complete strangers had become a way of life.

One particular time, I was invited to eat lunch at a restaurant with a senior pastor and some people from his congregation. We sat at a very long table because there were twelve of us. I was on one end and the pastor was on the other. We were all immersed in little clusters of conversation. All of a sudden the pastor said,

"Kathy, can I ask you something?"

All conversations ceased. All eyes turned to me.

"Sure, Pastor."

Because this was the first time he had spoken directly to me, I was expecting the simple exchanges of getting to know one another, such as: *Where are you from? How was your flight? Or even, How was your lunch?* Instead, this is what he asked me:

"Are you baptized in the Holy Spirit?"

An awkward silence engulfed the table. Many thoughts raced through my mind. *Am I before a jury here? Is everyone waiting for the right answer? Why would he ask me this? If I say, "Yes," am I in the club? If I say, "No," are they all going to lay hands on me right here at the table?*

I don't want to address the subject of baptism by the Holy Spirit here. What I *do* want to address is how we approach one another. Do we have sensitivity, gracious timing, and respect for another's beliefs? We are often more concerned with people's "spiritual state" than with trying to understand or get to know them. We don't know their background, their religion, their culture—we may not even know their names—yet we quickly present our agenda.

At that moment, I didn't feel that the pastor cared about *me*. In fact, I felt somewhat shamed. The only thought that came to my head and quickly out of my mouth was:

"Well, Pastor, are you asking me if I love well?"

He responded with a nervous laugh. I just smiled and went on in conversation, asking about him and his family. I knew my words to the pastor seemed pointed, but they simply were an overflow of what I had been reading in the Gospels and my recent frustration of how we express our Christianity.

As believers, we may be quick to give our thoughts on salvation, or doctrine, or even immorality, and what we say may be true and vital, but if we don't care about an individual's state of mind or heart, the person will certainly know it. You would be surprised how much more respect you get from someone when you really listen and show him you care.

Isn't it wonderful that God is a perfect gentleman? He is chivalrous and sensitive. He is love. And if we are going to bear His imprint, then we *must* be His love.

So often we make the mark of a Christian something quite different from what Jesus commanded and lived out. For example,

A priest might have asked:
"Are you going to confession and communion regularly?"

A Methodist or Episcopalian might have questioned:
"Are you volunteering in our soup kitchen?"

A Baptist might have wondered:
"Are you having your daily quiet time?"

(Have we officially offended everyone by now?) All of those things may be good things, but it is possible to be doing them all and yet *not* bear the imprint of Christ.

5. What did you learn from the above story that you could apply to your own life when approaching others?

_____

_____

Day 3

THE REAL DEAL

(Dee) Jim is a friend of mine who works with troubled youth. Through the help of God, he's found freedom from drugs and other prisons. Because Jim has a rough manner and poor grammar, people might easily dismiss him, but he is a true man of God, bearing the distinct imprint of a Christian. He stopped by one morning. With his usual carefree attitude, he plopped himself down on the couch. He noticed I was in the middle of writing and asked how he could pray for me. When I told him that Kathy and I had been working on a book about loving others as Jesus does, he grinned, saying,

> "Yeah, that's the real deal. When kids at the center ask me what Christians do, I go, 'They love on people.'"

> I smiled, loving Jim's concise description and wishing it were always true.

> Jim continued, "And then they ask me, 'Even the ones that make you wanna puke?'"

> Thoughts raced through my head, thinking of a few of the "hard-to-love" people in my life.

> Jim's face was filled with compassion as he reflected. "Dee, you can't imagine the junk thrown at these kids—at home they get cussed at, beat, and worse. . . . And so I tell them: 'Especially them. It's no big deal to love the easy ones. Love starts with the hard ones. That's where Jesus comes in.'"

Jesus is our standard, and it is a high one. He did not cling to His life but left His Father's throne and took on the form of a servant. He lived a life of love, always putting others first. He went to the cross because of love. He was "The Real Deal." However, *and this is crucial,* if you attempt to follow the model of Christ in your own strength, you will certainly fail. You must walk in His grace, trusting Him to live through you. This is what the apostles learned. When they tried on their own, they failed. But after receiving the Holy Spirit and walking in grace, they reflected the life of Christ.

The author of the letter we are studying is the apostle John, and he was certainly up close and personal with "The Real Deal." Jesus chose John to be part of His inner circle of three. John was the only disciple who didn't flee at the Crucifixion, and Jesus entrusted His mother, Mary, to him. The Lord chose John, of all the disciples, to remain alive, and then gave him the amazing vision of the end times, of Christ's return, and of the New Jerusalem. Charles Spurgeon calls him "the elect of the elect," the nearest, dearest, and closest fellowship with Christ in the flesh, the one who leaned his head on the breast of Jesus.

Prepare your heart by singing to the Lord, either from songs in Appendix B or other songs that express your adoration of Him.

6. Meditate on 1 John 1:1. Read John's breathless excitement and find the different senses that were involved in his being "up close and personal" with Jesus.

_____

_____

The following paintings by the masters are scenes from Jesus' life. John was there, in each case. Study the painting carefully and make observations. We hope to make you students of art, for art is another way to see spiritual truths. Then read the passage that tells what was heard, seen, or touched. Put yourself in John's place and describe what was happening and how he might have felt.

"CHRIST WASHING PETER'S FEET"
FORD MADOX BROWN (1821–1893)

7. What do you notice in the above painting?

_____ Jesus' head is bowed. Peter looks stern.

_____

_____

8. Read John 13:1–17 and put yourself in John's place. How did he hear, see, and feel the love of Jesus? What thoughts might have been going through his head?

_____

_____

"THE CRUCIFIXION"
PETER PAUL RUBENS (1577–1640)

9. Read John 19:25–27 and imagine yourself in John's place. What do you think he was feeling? How does he express it in 1 John 3:16–20?

_____

_____

10. What do you see in the above painting by Caravaggio on page 31? Note the other disciples and the expression of Jesus.

_____

_____

11. Though we often think only of Thomas in the above incident, this painting reminds us of John's words: "which we have looked at and our hands have touched" (1 John 1:1). Read John 20:24–31 and put yourself in John's place. What do you think he was feeling and thinking when this happened?

_____

_____

_____

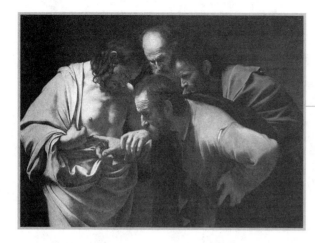

"DOUBTING THOMAS"
CARAVAGGIO (1573–1610)

12. Now, go back to the opening of 1 John and read 1 John 1:1–2 again. Observe all you can in this passage. Describe John's credentials and emotions.

_____

_____

13. Though we did not have the firsthand experiences with Jesus that John did, still, John makes some amazing promises in 1 John 1:3–4. There are three of them. Find them.

_____

_____

14. One of the secrets that will be made clearer through this study is that one of the ways we can see Jesus is through other believers, in whom He is reflected. We can love Jesus and be loved by Jesus through them. Write below about a recent time when you experienced real intimacy with the Lord or felt His love deeply through a time of sharing with other believers.

_____

_____

Review your memory passage.

Day 4

THE MOST IMPORTANT THING

(Dee) One of the patterns I have found in Scripture is that God *repeats* the most important things, such as telling us to love and to trust Him. We would *also* be wise to pay very close attention to the things that were said when time was running out, as with Jesus' seven last words on the cross. We ourselves tend to say the most important things when time is running out.

I was blessed to have a wonderful dad. Though his career held enormous responsibilities, family came first. He would often stress to me and my two sisters how much he wanted us to love one another. "I love you so much, but one day I'll be gone, so I want to know you are caring for each other." On my way to a speaking engagement in Dallas, I received a call that my dad had suffered a massive stroke. I flew to California to be at his side in the intensive care ward. For eight days I sat with him, wondering if he knew I was there. His eyes were closed, his breathing labored. Those eight days were some of the hardest and yet the most precious of my life.

Dad had always been a giant in my eyes: a man of integrity, a man of intellect, a man of strong opinions (not all of which I shared), but a man absolutely committed to his wife and three daughters. Now life was ebbing from him. He seemed so frail, so helpless. My mother, his bride of sixty-five years, sang him love songs, breaking my heart with:

"Let me call you Sweetheart, I'm in love with you . . ."

She was telling him the most important thing. She was telling him of her love for him. My sisters and I did the same.

One night, after a long day at the hospital, I went back to my parents' home. As I sat at Dad's desk, I was comforted to spy a gift I'd given to him one Father's Day. It was a clothbound journal, in which I had written a reason, on each page, why I loved him. Though it was several years old, there it was, right on his desk. I slipped it into my purse to read to him at the hospital. I didn't know when he would die, though it seemed likely it would be soon. I kept changing my return flight home. Finally, God gave me a peace about saying good-bye. With tears I pleaded with the Lord to give me a special moment with him, one in which Dad would open his eyes and hear me, *really hear me.*

When I walked into his room, I was overwhelmed because, for the first time, his eyes were open. When someone is prayed for so diligently, you know God is faithful to bring His abiding presence—especially at the end of his life. This is exactly what I sensed at my father's bedside. With tears streaming down my cheeks, I held his weakened hands, telling him the most important things—of my love, and of God's love for him. He was watching me intently. My adult son John sat by, watching, weeping, and praying.

"Mom," he said, "look at how his eyes are fixed on yours. He's hearing you."

I shared about Jesus once again, and then I read to him from the journal, telling him the reasons I loved him. I thanked him for his integrity, for his devotion to Mother, for his enthusiasm for life, for introducing me to the classics, for taking me to faraway places, for loving dogs, for *always* being there when I needed him. From one of the pages, I read:

Thank you, Dad, for always being at the gate whenever I came home. I knew I could count on you. As soon as I walked out of the plane, I'd see your eyes intent on the door, watching for me. Then your handsome face would light up and you'd cry: "There she is!" Then you'd laugh and open your arms for our great hug.

I began to sob.

"Please, Daddy, *please, please.* Be at the gate."

Those were the last words I spoke to him. He died two days later.

What do we say when time is running out? The most important thing.

It is remarkable to consider the day we were scheduled to begin writing *Living in Love with Jesus*. We planned to begin on September 11, 2001, at 9 A.M. We had gone to my cabin in Door County, Wisconsin, for time away from the world, where we could really concentrate. I was all set up and ready to go: I had positioned our working table so it faced the waves of Green Bay, the coffee was brewing, and the fire was crackling in the fireplace. For four days we would write. I was putting on my jacket to go get Kathy at her hotel, when the phone rang.

(Kathy) I had turned on the television as I was getting ready to take a shower. There it was: an airplane flying into one of the World Trade Towers. I was horrified. I began to weep. I called Dee to tell her to turn on her TV. We quickly hung up. The other plane hit the second tower. I sat on my bed, completely paralyzed. My beloved city was crumbling right before my eyes. A knock at the door awakened me from the nightmare that I wished *were* just a dream. It was Dee. I fell into her arms and we both sobbed. All we could do was cry out to Jesus. We continued to watch the news together. As the day wore on, we learned what had actually happened: An evil had descended on this nation, taking with it thousands of lives. Story upon story unfolded of people calling from hijacked planes and burning buildings.

Sons calling mothers to say, "I love you."

Sisters calling brothers to say, "I love you. Tell Mom and Dad I love them."

Men calling wives to say, "I love you—tell the kids I love them. Take care of each other."

What do we say at the end? The most important thing.

It's remarkable that as Jesus neared the Cross, He wanted to convey the same message as those who were about to die on that tragic September day: "Let them know that I love them, and love one another."

15. Turn to the Gospel of John, Chapter 13.

    A. In John 13:33a, how does Jesus let the disciples know His time is running out?

    _____

    B. In John 13:34b how does He remind them of His love? What command does He give?

    _____

    _____

Do you see? He loves us. And we are not only to *tell* others of His love, we are to *be* His love, *give* His love, *live* His love. We are to bear this imprint to one another. Jesus was very clear about this.

C. By what sign, according to John 13:35, will men know we are His disciples?

_____

When you brush a crayon across a leaf, you can see its veins, its stem, and its unique shape. The identity of the tree that birthed that leaf, that gave it life, is distinctive.

What is the imprint of a believer? Is it obvious who gave us birth? Can they see His hands, His eyes, His heart, His love? When people brush up against us, are they intrigued and inquisitive about the source of our love? Do they recognize Jesus?

If the church were a heart, its current failure to love is like a massive heart attack. We, as the arteries, get clogged with judgment, hate, pride, and gossip. How can His lifeblood flow through us toward each other, let alone into a world so desperate for the love of Christ?

It is no coincidence that the message gets muddied and the imprint faded.

It is no coincidence that the message gets distorted and the imprint counterfeited.

(Dee) I went through some of the same struggles Kathy did when I began my journey into Christianity. So many messages came at me, and I was trying to discern who was "right" and what was most important. God ministered to me through an eloquent little book entitled *The Mark of a Christian* by Francis Schaeffer, a man who was a prophet in his time, cutting to the core, discerning where the church was headed. Schaeffer explained that the mark of a Christian is Jesus, but the way the world sees Jesus in us is through love. How intriguing that love, and not doctrine, is the sign of authenticity to the world. Francis Schaeffer explains:

> *The church is to judge whether a man is a Christian on the basis of his doctrine . . . and then his credible profession of faith. . . . But we cannot expect the world to judge that way, because the world cares nothing about doctrine . . .*[2]

As believers, we *must* care about doctrine, and John will eventually give us some doctrinal tests to discern a true believer from a counterfeit. But since the world does not care about doctrine, they measure our authenticity on the basis of love.

16. Ask the Lord to make you more sensitive today to being His love to the people in your life. Tomorrow, write down any opportunities you seized.

_____

_____

A NEW COMMANDMENT

Jesus has clearly stated that the two most important commandments are to love God and to love our neighbor. However, in John 13:34, we also hear Him refer to a "new command." John talks about this new commandment again in his letter. His words seem almost like a riddle. Read 1 John 2 as an overview.

17. Read 1 John 2:7–11. Now focus on verse 7. The old command is to love our *neighbor*, yet John gives a *new* command to love our *brother*. So, when John says this is *not* a new command, but an old, what do you think he means? And when he says it *is* a new command, what does he mean?

_____

_____

Dr. Schaeffer stressed that not only did Jesus *command* us to be His love, He *prayed* we would be His love in John 17. This passage has been called His "High Priestly Prayer." *When* did Jesus pray this? Near the end of His life on earth, when time was running out, just before He was betrayed. We must listen carefully. In this prayer He again tells us what will cause the world to believe, to *know* that the Father sent the Son.

18. For three years, Jesus has lived under a death sentence, which, in John 17, is just days away.

   A. For whom is Jesus praying, according to John 17:9?

   _____

   B. Who else did Jesus pray for, according to John 17:20?

   _____

   C. What did He pray, according to John 17:21a?

   _____

   D. And why, according to John 17:21b?

   _____

   E. How does He repeat this in John 17:23?

   _____

It is possible to "be one" without being the same. Though we must agree on central truths (that Jesus is God incarnate, that we are saved through faith alone in His shed blood, and that we are to live for Him), we may disagree on peripheral issues. We may prefer different styles of worship, different modes of baptism, and different entertainment choices. We may even disagree on certain peripheral doctrinal issues. (Kathy and Dee don't agree about everything!) We can disagree, but we *must* do so in love. Schaeffer writes:

> *What divides and severs true Christian groups and Christians—what leaves a bitterness that can last for 20, 30, or 40 years (or for 50 or 60 years in a son's memory)—is not the issue of doctrine or belief which caused the differences in the first place. Invariably it is the lack of love—and the bitter things that are said by true Christians in the midst of differences. These stick in the mind like glue.*[3]

19. What are some ways that believers in this world are divided and lacking in love for one another in their homes, communities, and within the body of Christ?

_____

_____

Unless we genuinely love each other, unless we truly care for each other, unless we are living in harmony, *the world will not believe.* There is so much dissension out there: quarreling, misunderstanding, and belittling. The world lives like this. The world lives without hope. We do much of the same. Why would anybody *without* Jesus want our life *with* Jesus if it looks the same? Believe me, they're watching. *We* watch! Why wouldn't they be watching?

Everybody wants the real deal. And when you show the real deal, the purity of love, it is hard to resist. There is no moving toward God without love. If we who bear His name do not love, Jesus tells us the world will dismiss *Him.* This is sobering, because we all know Christians who do not bear this imprint, and each of us at one time or another could step to the front of that line.

Jesus gives us *two* commands about loving others: We are to love our neighbor as ourselves; we are to love our *brother* as Christ loved us. Both love commands are vital, and both kinds of love are to be seen in the mark of a Christian. It certainly would be ugly to love *just* other believers and not our neighbor. Yet Scripture stresses that there is something terribly important about loving our *brother.* When unbelievers witnessed the great love between the believers in the book of Acts, when they saw how they took care of their poor, when they saw how strong the bond was between believers, they were drawn to Jesus as well. Again and again it is repeated in the New Testament that it is absolutely vital that we, in the body of Christ, show love for one another. See these dual commands, including the emphasis on the new command:

> *Therefore, as we have opportunity, let us do good to all people, especially to those who belong to the family of believers.* (Galatians 6:10)

Francis Schaeffer explains:

> *Jesus turns to the world and says, "I've something to say to you. On the basis of my authority, I give you a right: you may judge whether or not an individual is a Christian on the basis of the love he shows to all Christians."*

We are not to choose between loving all men as ourselves and loving Christians in a special way . . . but we can understand how overwhelmingly important it is that all men be able to see an observable love for those with whom we have these special ties.

. . . We must be very careful at this point, however. We may be true Christians, really born-again Christians, and yet fail in love toward other Christians. As a matter of fact, to be completely realistic, it is stronger than this. There will be times (and let us say it with tears), there will be times when we will fail in our love toward each other as Christians.

The point is that it is possible to be a Christian without showing the mark, but if we expect non-Christians to know that we are Christians, we must show the mark.[4]

20. Name some ways that you can show the love of Christ to the other women in this Bible study group. Name also some thoughts and actions you must avoid.

_____

_____

The mark of a Christian is Jesus in us or, as J. B. Phillips puts it, "the stamp of Christ." The way the world *sees* this stamp is through the distinctive *love* of Christ.

How can we be certain to show the mark? How can we be transformed?

This is the exciting part, for John's first letter could be called Christianity 101, giving us basic principles that can transform us into beautiful women of God. If you are a man doing this study, the principles will work for you too. These four transforming principles are the ways the love of Christ can flow through you. His love is different from the world's love and is based on:

Light,
Death,
Truth,
Mercy.

Have you ever experienced a sunrise from an airplane? It is a breathtaking way to start the day. Looking out our windows before takeoff, the sky is normally blue-black. The city is sleeping. As we soar above the clouds, the light of the majestic orange-yellow sun transforms *everything*. What a beautiful sight. As the minutes pass by, we are certain this same light will stream into kitchen windows, set farmlands ablaze, and glisten like diamonds on city skyscrapers. Tiny churches and grand cathedrals will become iridescent because of the penetrating light shining through their stained-glass windows.

The sun definitely touches the world with a unique beauty. The light of Jesus Christ can do the same through us. We can touch the world with the colors of His love.

Next week we will look more carefully at the "blacks and whites" of 1 John, and see how these bold principles can help us be transformed into women who bear the stamp of Christ. As we practice them, we will see how they make the imprint of Christ stronger in us.

Pray through 1 John 3:18–20 for yourself:

Dear children, let us not love with words or tongue but with actions and in truth. This then is how we know that we belong to the truth, and how we set our hearts at rest in His presence whenever our hearts condemn us. For God is greater than our hearts, and He knows everything.

21. What do you think you will remember most from this week's lesson? Why? How could you apply it?

_____

_____

PRAYER TIME

How vital it is to carry out this love right within this group. Cluster in groups of no larger than four and ask each woman to vulnerably lift up whatever is concerning her the most in her life right now. Then the women can support her with sentence prayers. When there is a silence, another woman can bravely lift up her need. If you cannot bring yourself to honestly share, you can say, "I have an unspoken request." Your prayer time might look something like this:

Connie: I wish I could be closer to my daughter, Amy, but she seems to shut me out.

Anne: Lord, I know it would please You to have Connie and Amy grow closer. Please give Connie great wisdom and sensitivity this week.

Joan: Please help Connie see some bricks come down from that wall.

Ellen: Yes, Lord.

Silence

Anne: I have an unspoken request.

Joan: Be with Anne, Lord. You know her needs. Please give her strength and wisdom.

Connie: Yes, Lord.

BLACK AND WHITE

(Kathy)

I have shared in concert and expressed in my books my love for the Baker boys: Logan, Jordan, and Jared. They are six, four, and two, and a delight to my soul. I stay with their family often, and the guest bedroom is right off the kitchen, so, needless to say, I don't need an alarm clock. One morning Jared, the two-year-old, burst through my door and hopped onto my bed.

"Coli, Coli, wake up!"

As he bounced up and down on the mattress, I groggily reached for him and drew him close. He squirmed his way out, but I got enough of a morning hug to start my day.

"Get up, Coli! I want to show you my Spider-Man play."

I thought, *Spider-Man? This should be interesting.* As always, I was drawn by his sweetness. I dragged myself out of bed, grinning in anticipation. He raced down the hall with just a t-shirt on and no bottoms, delighted that I was following him. When we entered his bedroom it was completely dark except for a little flashlight he had rigged up to the bedpost. It was shining on two chairs that he put side by side for the audience (his mom and me). Allyson and I sat down with exaggerated excitement. He then stood right in front of us and spoke with all the theatrics of a magician. He whispered intensely:

"Get ready . . . to be amazed."

Allyson and I looked at each other and wanted to burst out laughing. When I left the Bakers' house I reminisced. It's always a precious time for me. Jared's statement kept playing over and over again in my head. With all the responsibilities that come upon me each day, I could easily become anxious and discouraged. But when I rest in God, placing my trust once again in Him and His promises, I hear Jared's words ring out to me, as if from the mouth of God:

Get ready to be amazed.

Then, just a little while later, I was reading in Habakkuk, and found this:

Look at the nations and watch—
and be utterly amazed.
For I am going to do something in your days
that you would not believe,
even if you were told.
(Habakkuk 1:5)

In the same way, John begins his letter with some huge promises—promises that we might have trouble believing, and yet, when we look at the Lord's track record, we have to admit, He *is* an amazing God. He is also a mysterious God, and often His ways of accomplishing His will surprise us. That was true in the book of Habakkuk, and it is also true in the book of 1 John.

Remember who is writing 1 John. There were plenty of times when Christ amazed him. John was there, for example, when Christ stopped the storm. This was just the beginning of John's amazement at the power of Jesus:

"Christ in the Storm on the Sea of Galilee"
Rembrandt (Painted in 1633)

John lived, according to historians, longer than any of the disciples. He was the one who was given the amazing revelation of the end times.

"St. John"
Titian (Painted in 1535)

Charles Spurgeon wrote:

Remember what order of man John was, that disciple whom Jesus loved, whose head had leaned on Jesus' bosom. . . . This is he who at one time saw the pierced heart of the well-beloved pouring forth blood and water; and at another beheld the Lion of the tribe of Judah prevail to take the book and loose the seven seals thereof.[1]

Jesus also transformed John. He knows, from firsthand experience, that the principles he is giving us in his letter actually work.

This week we will be doing an overview of the black-and-white principles in this letter, which, at first glance, can seem harsh and difficult. Yet, stay with us, and,

Get ready to be amazed.

VIDEO NOTES FOR WEEK 3
BLACK AND WHITE

Thoughts I want to remember:

I can have an intimate relationship with Jesus if I live according to these principles.

1. Some of John's black-and-white statements are:

Whoever claims to live in him must walk as ___Jesus___ did. (1 John 2:6)

No one who lives in him keeps on sinning. (1 John 3:6)

He who does what is sinful is of the ___devil___. (1 John 3:8)

Anyone who does not do what is right is not a child of God. (1 John 3:10b)

Anyone who hates his brother is a ___murderer___. (1 John 3:15)

Whoever does not love does not know God. (1 John 4:8)

2. *The man who is really God's son does not ___practice___ sin, for God's nature is in him, for good, and such a ___heredity___ is incapable of sin.* (1 John 3:8–9 PHILLIPS)

3. We become like the One who gave us ___birth___.

4. *The Life Direction of:*

GOD'S CHILDREN   SATAN'S CHILDREN

Live in light.   Live in _darkness_

Die to self.   Live _for_ self.

Speak the truth.   Speak _lies_ .

Plan good and carry it out.   Plan _evil_ and carry it out.

5. Our love and our hatred not only reveal if we are in the light or in the darkness, but actually _contribute_ to the light or darkness in which we already are. (John Stott)

6. *But if anyone obeys his word, God's love is truly made* _complete_ *in him.* (1 John 2:5a)

If we love one another, God lives in us and his love is made _complete_ *in us.* (1 John 4:12b)

Whoever lives in love lives in God, and God in him. In this way, love is made _____ *among us so that we will have confidence on the day of judgment, because in this world we are like him.* (1 John 4:16b–17)

7. The more you walk in the light,

     the stronger the _light_ of Christ will become in you.

The more you die to yourself,

     the more Christ will _live_ in you.

The more you live by the truth,

     the more you will be _set free_ to be like Christ.

The more you love your brother,

     the more God's love will be made _complete_ in you.

8. The label "Christian" is pretty easy to attain. The label "_holiness_" is much harder.

9. *And his commands are not* _burdensome_ . (1 John 5:3b) *— — — They set us free*

10. God is _light_ , so we *must* stay in the light.

Jesus laid down His _life_ , so we *must* die to ourselves.

God is _truth_ , so we *must* live by the truth.

God is _mercy_, so we *must* be merciful.

ICEBREAKER *(Hear from several women for each question.)*

1. In one sentence, name one way God has amazed you.

_____

2. What stood out to you from the video? Why?

_____

Day 1

THE BATTLE

Can you remember when you first discovered who Jesus was? What an awakening! Your heart and mind were opened to a whole new world. You started thinking way beyond earthly things. For some of us, it was almost a euphoric state. Each new day held a different promise. We finally understood the reason for the deep ache in our souls. We finally understood our loneliness—it was for our Maker. Answers to some of our questions were revealed.

For many of us, however, a time comes when the reality of life sets in again. We wake from our honeymoon, open the curtains, and observe the true state of affairs:

Life is still hard.
We still get lonely.
People still do ugly things.
There is still pain.
There are still injustices.
Evil still pervades our world.

It can all seem so discouraging. Our initial passion wanes. We begin to lose the enthusiasm and strength we once held in our hearts to take the high and narrow road.

We knew God would lead us when He asked us to follow Him, but we didn't know we would follow Him through some dark places. Our immaturity led us to believe that the hard would get less hard, and the easy would get easier.

So, subtly and slowly, we find ourselves questioning all the things we so earnestly embraced in the beginning. We find ourselves asking:

Now, why do I want to be holy?

The cost is great. Our flesh wages war against everything God stands for. We just don't know if we have it in us. We want to be His, but do we want to be holy? Instead of pushing on with the passion that once drove us toward the high places, we become complacent and settle into a comfortable nest of mediocrity. We no longer dream of flying. We'd rather stay put. We think:

I don't want to work that hard.
I don't want to be that challenged.
I don't want to be that honest.

All we can see is the cost. The wonder is gone. We are no longer prepared, each day, to be amazed.

God knows us. He made us. He knows we have unfaithful hearts and that we will lose the excitement of our first love. So, thousands of years ago, He appointed John to write to you and to me.

1. Review and list the amazing promises John makes in 1 John 1:3–4.

   _____
   _____

2. Find and note below a few other promises (among many) that John gives for those who long to be holy:

   A. 1 John 1:7_____

   B. 1 John 2:5_____

   C. 1 John 2:10_____

   D. 1 John 2:14_____

   E. 1 John 2:28_____

However, despite what the last verse promises, when you first read through John's letter you may find that instead of increasing your confidence, it makes you feel woefully inadequate. Instead of inspiring you to greater heights, it makes you feel like giving up! He seems to say that if you are a *true* child of God you will:

always stay in the light,
always obey,
always love your brother,
always embrace the truth.

3. Skim 1 John and find a few examples of John's black-and-white polarities. We've gotten you started:

If we claim to have fellowship with him yet walk in the darkness, we lie and do not live by the truth (1 John 1:6). _____

_____

_____

_____

_____

_____

_____

_____

_____

Each of us knows we have failed at every single one of the above. So we wonder:

> *Is he kidding?*
> *I wander in the darkness a lot. Am I damned?*
> *Am I "of the devil" because I sin every day?*

It could make you run for the hills. However, John is not saying we will *not* sin. So what is he saying? We'll begin to look at that tomorrow.

Begin learning your memory passage.

DEAR CHILDREN, I WRITE THESE THINGS TO YOU SO YOU WILL NOT SIN

On first appearance, John's letter almost seems to be implying that a *true* child of God will never sin. Yet John makes it clear that we all are sinful.

4. Read 1 John 1:8–10 and find what he says about our sinfulness in each verse:

v. 8 _____

_____

v. 9 _____

_____

v. 10 _____

_____

Essential to winning the fight is truly grasping our own depravity. Paul puts it like this: "When I want to do good, evil is right there with me" (Romans 7:21b). If we have received Jesus, we have His nature in us. However, we also have our old nature, and it fights to survive.

5. As you look over your own life in just the last twenty-four hours, as you allow the holy light of God to search your soul, how can you see your own sinfulness, your own depravity? (You don't need to share this in the group, but it is essential to victory to understand where you are weak. *Early detection of sin* is a gift, just as is early detection of cancer. You can allow the Spirit to overcome the sin before the sin overcomes you.)

_____

_____

_____

6. Why, according to 1 John 2:1a, is John writing these things?

_____

7. But what wonderful provision is given to us when we *do* sin according to 1 John 2:1b? What are we told that Jesus does?

_____

_____

If you know this chorus, you could sing it in praise to God in your time alone with Him. Or, meditate on the words.

> *What can wash away my sin?*
> *Nothing but the blood of Jesus;*
> *What can make me whole again?*
> *Nothing but the blood of Jesus.*
>
> *O precious is the flow*
> *That makes me white as snow;*
> *No other fount I know,*
> *Nothing but the blood of Jesus.*
> (Public Domain)

8. According to 1 John 2:1–2, why is Jesus qualified to speak to the Father in our defense?

_____

9. The nature we feed is the nature that grows. Each time you give in to the sinful nature, each time you feed the sinful nature with trash, it thrives. What warning and what promise does Paul give in Romans 8:13?

_____

_____

Over the next two weeks, as we look carefully at what it means to walk in the light, you will learn what it means to walk in repentance. We are in a battle—with the enemy, with our own sinful nature, and with the difficult circumstances of life all on one side. But we also have a mighty God within us, who is eager to help us win. Beth Moore has said we need to "plan our victories." Consider your answer to question 10 below, and look at where you are weak. Whether it is gossiping, a failure to spend time with the Lord, pride, overeating, a failure to love your neighbor—plan your victory!

10. How might you "plan your victory" in an area where you are weak today? (Pray, asking for wisdom, and be still before God. Then write down your strategy.)

_____

_____

_____

_____

The above plan will help you in your battle against the sin, but if you do sin, remember not to deny it or hide it. Quickly confess it and turn right back to the light.

Continue learning your memory passage.

Day 3

A CHILD REFLECTS THE ONE WHO GAVE HER BIRTH

(Dee) Kathy has many of the wonderful characteristics of her mother, Josephine. Her mother was smart and organized. She was a great administrator and delegated well. I see this clearly in Kathy. Even while we are working, she is continually adding things to her "to do" list. She keeps a dozen balls in the air, like so many fragile ornaments, with very few crashing and breaking. She is like her mother in this.

Kathy has also admitted to sharing some negative characteristics of her mother. Josephine liked things "just so." Kathy has shared with me that her mother liked the towels folded a certain way before they were put in the closet. She wanted the carrots cut a certain way before they were put in the salad. She wanted the Christmas ornaments placed exactly in the right boxes before they were put back in the attic. It drove Kathy crazy. Now she admits she drives those close to her a little crazy with the same compulsive tendencies.

Since I have grown close to Kathy I see that, like Josephine, she is a perfectionist. Even in the midst of intense writing days, it is not unusual for her to pick a piece of lint from my sweater, push my bangs back, or mention an ink smudge on my finger. She notices everything. Her office is beautiful, classy, and immaculate. Every drawer is in order. Every closet is perfectly organized. Even her attic is dust-free. Sometimes I'll catch her getting way too particular about some small detail, and I'll say, "Okay, Josephine."

She'll immediately take the hint and say, "I know, I know. I'm sorry."

We tend to reflect the image of our parents, the good and the bad. Ezekiel 16:44 quotes the familiar proverb: "Like mother, like daughter."

KATHY AND JOSEPHINE TROCCOLI

A child tends to reflect, genetically, the physical and often the personality traits of his parents. This is true in a spiritual sense as well. If the consistent direction of your life is to walk in the darkness and to hate your brother, you should, indeed, be concerned if you are really a child of God. If the consistent life direction of someone who claims to be a Christian does not reflect the life of God, he or she may be a counterfeit, and John warns us to be alert to the counterfeit "believers" among us so we are not led astray.

There *are* wolves in sheep's clothing who may lead us astray with false teaching, may marry and exploit our daughters, and may devour us. We must look for fruit, and if it is not there, we must be alert to the counterfeit. We must recognize when someone is not the real thing, and we should be more concerned with *our* being the real thing.

This doesn't mean we will never fail. We are depraved and we *will* sin. But it does mean, as children of God, because He is perfection, because He is love, and because He is holy, we should reflect the One who gave us spiritual birth.

11. Meditate on the following passage:

> *The man who lives a consistently good life is a good man, as surely as God is good. But the man whose life is habitually sinful is spiritually a son of the devil, for the devil is behind all sin,*

as he always has been. Now the Son of God came to earth with the express purpose of liquidating the devil's activities. The man who is really God's son does not practice sin, for God's nature is in him, for good, and such a heredity is incapable of sin. (1 John 3:8–9 PHILLIPS)

A. Who is behind all good? Who is behind all sin?

_____

B. Why did the Son of God come to earth?

_____

C. The child of God has God's nature in him. What do you learn about this heredity?

_____

> God's child does not make a practice of sin. That is such a powerful statement. He knows we will sin. He understands our capabilities. But His desire is that we do not have a "life direction" of it.

That is what Jesus meant when He said to the adulteress, "Go and sin no more." *Don't let it be your life choice.* We *will* fail. John makes that clear. But we absolutely must learn to walk in repentance, every day. Our life direction must be the light, and the moment we are aware we have moved into the shadows, we *must* repent and come back to the light. That is how we nurture the amazing heredity within us. That is how we begin to reflect the imprint of the Lord.

(Dee) When our firstborn, J. R., was a little boy, we had some new neighbors over for the evening. In the middle of dinner, J. R. asked:

"Do you guys love Jesus?"

There was an awkward silence. When no one answered, J. R. asked:

"Well, do you love the devil?"

We laughed, and it was welcome comic relief. Then our guest responded:

"Are those my only choices?"

I am realizing, as I comprehend 1 John, how J. R.'s simplicity actually cut to the truth. John is saying that we reflect the one who gave us birth—and yes, we only have two choices for spiritual parenthood. John's letter makes it clear that either our parent is the Father of Light or the father of darkness. As we mature, we become more and more like the one who gave us birth. This truth permeates John's letter.

12. Read 1 John 3 slowly and find examples of the truth that permeate John's letter: Either we reflect God or we reflect the evil one.

_____

_____

_____

If you know the following chorus, sing it in your time with God:

Beloved, let us love one another,
for love is of God, and everyone who loveth
is born of God, and knoweth God.
He that loveth not,
knoweth not God, for God is love.
Beloved, let us love one another.
First John, four, seven and eight.

_____

© Maranatha Music. Administered by The Copyright Co. All Rights Reserved. Used by Permission.

Day 4

THE SECRET TO LIVING IN LOVE WITH JESUS

(Kathy) Now by this point, you must be reading this saying, *Okay, Kathy and Dee, that's just what I'll do. Yeah, right.* It's like when I was thirty pounds overweight, my thin sister said, "Well, Kath, just eat less." But you know what? It was the truth. And as I learned to eat less, to stay within the boundaries of healthy eating, I found that I arrived at a place of rejoicing. The narrow road became a beautiful one.

(Dee) I gave my life to Christ shortly after our firstborn's first birthday. I did not have any idea how to be a godly mother, and it took some time to learn. When J. R. was three, he ruled our home with his strong will. One Sunday he was tearing through the sanctuary when an older woman opened her big Bible and got right in my face. She said, "It says right here that if you refuse to discipline your son you will ruin his life!"

I remember thinking, *Wow—that was rude!* But you know what? She was speaking the truth to me. And as I learned to obey "the blacks and whites," I arrived at a place of rejoicing. Not only did we begin to have peace in our home, but our child, and the four siblings who followed him, grew up to love and serve the Lord. (Certainly, it is God's grace that produced this; but I also know that if I had not learned to discipline my children, it is very unlikely that they would be walking with the Lord.)

We understand how all of this sounds so great and godly. As a matter of fact, it can seem unattainable because of our human frailty. But remember: The Spirit that raised Jesus from the dead lives in us. We *can* do all things. He will supply what He demands.

Read this next quotation from John Stott carefully, for it is a deep thought, but it's vital to understanding 1 John, and to understanding the secret of living in love with Jesus:

Our love and our hatred not only reveal if we are in the light or in the darkness, but actually contribute to the light or darkness in which we already are.[2]

13. Kathy and Dee each shared an example of where God's truth was hard, at first, but when obeyed, brought them into a place of rejoicing. Can you share an example like this from your own life?

_____

_____

Review your memory passage.

14. In the following verses, find the promise of perfection or completion, and then, the condition.

A. 1 John 2:5a

Promise:_____

Condition:_____

B. 1 John 4:12

Promise:_____

Condition:_____

C. 1 John 4:16–17

Promise:_____

Condition:_____

As we begin to understand John's black-and-white statements, we see the power in them to transform us into reflections of the Lord. Do you see?

Because God is light
        we *must* stay in the light.
Because Jesus laid down His life
        we *must* die to ourselves.
Because God is truth,
        we *must* live by the truth.
Because God is mercy,
        we *must* be merciful.

Here is the exciting part. We *will* have victory over our condemning hearts, over the lies of the enemy, and over a faded and colorless life, *if* we:

> stay in the light,
> die to ourselves,
> live by the truth,
> and show mercy.

The more you walk in the light, the stronger the light of Christ will become in you.
The more you die to yourself, the more Christ will live in you.
The more you live by truth, the more you will be set free to be like Christ.
The more you love your brother, the more you will show the mercy of Christ.

Choosing a life direction of the above things,

the stronger the imprint of Jesus will be in you.

Day 5

ANCIENT OF FOES

We cherish the opportunity that God has given us to share His life with you and to pray over you. Every day many of us deal with anxieties and fears that make us "lose our way" and doubt His love for us. It is wonderful to see women light up when we speak God's very own words over them.

> *You are the object of His affection.*
> *He has you engraved on the palms of His hands.*
> *You are His Beloved.*
> *How great is the love the Father has lavished upon you!*

What a privilege to be sharing with you, from Scripture, the glorious promises and portraits of His love. We see the longing, the hunger in your eyes, for within each of us, dark voices whisper, taunting:

> *You don't deserve to be loved.*
> *No one could know your darkest secrets and still love you.*
> *You're such a fraud.*
> *You keep blowing it. What's the point?*

Where do you think these thoughts come from?

He is called "the father of lies." He is known as "the accuser of the brethren." He is our enemy, Satan himself. In order to live in love with Jesus, not only do we need to win the battle over our own sin nature, we must win the battle over the enemy. How? By spotting his lies.

He wants us to doubt God's mercies. He wants us to doubt God's love. He plainly just wants us to doubt God. Soon we find ourselves thinking:

Does He really know what is best for me?
Can I really trust Him?
Surely He knows I'm not going to be able to live out a life of holiness.

It seems like an awful lot of hard work for little return.

We hesitate. We wonder if it will be worth it.

As women we often let our hearts lead us. But our sensitivity can also be used against us, and the enemy has done that time and time again. One of his favorite strategies is to attack our confidence in God by playing on our emotions and fears. As our doubts grow, our ability to resist temptation weakens. Soon we may begin to wonder if we really know Him, if we are really capable of living the Christian life, or if we can, indeed, overcome all that is in the world.

15. Can you think of a situation in the last few weeks when you doubted your ability to live a life of holiness, or when you wondered if you could really trust God's heart? If so, when was it? (You don't have to share it in the group.)

_____

16. What promise does John make in 1 John 4:4?

_____

If you know the following praise chorus, sing it in your time alone with God:

Greater is He that is in me
Greater is He that is in me
Greater is He that is in me
Than he that is in the world

John longs to equip us to overcome the evil one, and he gives us strategies to do that.

17. What strategies can you find for overcoming the deceit of the evil one in the following passages? (Hint: The deceit is in the first verse; the strategy to overcome is in the second verse.)

A. 1 John 1:8–9 _____

_____

B. 1 John 2:4–5 _____

_____

C. 1 John 2:9–10 _____

_____

18. Who is coming and what will precede him, according to 1 John 2:18?

_____

_____

"Many antichrists" can be interpreted as "a spirit of antichrist" at work in the world. You will find the lies of the enemy everywhere: on talk shows, in the public classroom, and in the mouths and minds of those who do not know God. Jesus wants us to walk on His bridge of truth to get us to the high places. But, like termites, the deception of the enemy has burrowed itself into our bridge. We are now vulnerable to the elements, the unexpected storms of life. The enemy knows these are coming, so he erodes our confidence in the Lord, causing our bridge of truth to tremble.

How can we defeat the enemy? We *must* pour God's truth into our souls, every day, throughout the day. We do not have to wait for someone to teach us, for the Holy Spirit of Truth is eager to teach us, if only we seek Him with open hearts.

19. In the following passage, John is not saying we cannot have teachers, for he himself is teaching, but is commenting on the lie that we cannot interpret the Scriptures for ourselves but must have someone interpret them for us. What does he say in 1 John 2:26–28?

_____

_____

Not only must we pour truth into our souls, we must be alert to the lies that are all around us. There are false teachers and counterfeit Christians. There is also "a spirit of antichrist" at work in the world.

20. The following are a few of the ways to recognize this spirit. You may not see all of the following signs in one person or viewpoint, but you will see some. What are they?

A. 1 John 2:22–23 _____

_____

B. 1 John 3:7–10 _____

_____

C. 1 John 4:1–3 _____

_____

D. 1 John 4:5–6 _____

_____

21. What have you learned this week that stood out to you and can help you live a victorious life?

_____

_____

PRAYER TIME

Cluster in small groups. Look at your answers to questions 10 and 20. Lift up one of these answers and allow the women to support you in this, that you really will be empowered to carry out what you plan to do. Your time in prayer might look something like this:

Connie: My strategy against gossip is to recognize it before I say it, and either be silent or say something else.

Anne: Lord, please remind Connie before a word is on her tongue, and help her be silent.

Joan: Give her joy as she sees victory in this area.

Ellen: Yes, Lord.

(Silence)

Ellen: I learned that the black-and-whites can bring me joy—help me to remember that when I don't want to discipline my two-year-old. Help me keep the boundaries I've set with him.

Joan: Yes, Lord, please give Ellen strength when it seems easier to ignore Ben.

Connie: Yes, Lord.

CLOTHED IN LIGHT:

Week 4: WALKING IN THE DARK

Week 5: WALKING IN THE LIGHT

GOD IS LIGHT *and no shadow of darkness can exist in him.*
(1 JOHN 1:5B PHILLIPS)

WALKING IN THE DARK

(Kathy)

I remember walking slowly through the Metropolitan Museum of Art in New York City, in awe of the talent God had bestowed upon man. I stood before a painting of Adam and Eve, and shuddered at the ominous presence of evil in the serpent wrapped tightly around the tree. I could almost hear the conversation that happened that day in the garden. "Did God *really* say?" "Are you sure?" How often *I* have been tempted to listen to those words. But Satan is always pulling a fast one. He wants us to doubt God. Why? So he can wreak havoc in our lives. So he can bring unimaginable pain into our days here on earth.

One of my favorite lines I have ever written is in a song called "At Your Mercy."

> *It only takes a moment's time for me to somehow cross the line*
> *where I can wind up roaming in the dark.*
> *Satan is a liar, I know he can start a fire*
> *then go tearing everything I have apart.*

This line comes to me often, especially as God is allowing me the wonderful privilege of ministering more and more deeply to women. We must always weigh what our choices will do to the lives of other people. If we fall, what will be the consequences? We need to ask, *If I choose this, what will happen?* Once when Dee and I were speaking, a woman asked us: "How *does* God convict you? How do you *know*?" When I am convicted by the Holy Spirit, I get that "holy twist." I feel a flush, almost like riding on a roller coaster.

(Dee) In the same way, I experience, nearly every day, that "holy twist" when I am about to say something I shouldn't say, watch something I shouldn't watch, or eat something I shouldn't eat. I am learning to recognize that uncomfortable feeling as a friend. It was kindness that caused God to entreat Cain, and when He entreats us, it is a gift, just as the pain we feel when we touch something hot is a gift. If we ignore it, we are being *so* foolish, for we may do permanent damage. Usually that uncomfortable feeling comes through my conscience, but I have found that as I immerse myself in His Word, His Spirit often brings a verse to my mind:

I reach for a potato chip and I think, *"Don't give the devil a foothold"* (Ephesians 4:27).
(I rejoice, later, because I resisted!)

A lonely person comes across my path and I think, *"Don't shut up your compassions"* (1 John 3:17b KJV).

(If I obey, His love is made complete in me.)

I am irritated and an unkind look or word flows out, and I don't want to admit my sin. Then I think, *"God opposes the proud but gives grace to the humble"* (James 4:6b).

(If I obey, He blesses my relationship with that person and fills me with joy.)

God promises us that if we respond to His rebuke, He will pour out His heart to us. He will make His thoughts known to us (Proverbs 1:23)! He also warns us that if we refuse, our hearts harden, our ears grow deaf, and we move into a downward spiral. It happened to Cain, and it can happen to us. The consequences of walking in the dark are huge, and we are so foolish to ignore His soft whispers.

VIDEO NOTES FOR WEEK 4
WALKING IN THE DARK

Thoughts I want to remember:

_____

_____

_____

1. *Do not be like Cain, who belonged to the evil one and murdered his* _____.
   (1 John 3:12)

2. *So Cain was very* _____, *and his face was downcast.* (Genesis 4:5b)

3. *Then the LORD said to Cain, "Why are you angry? Why is your face downcast? If you do what is* _____, *will you not be accepted?* (Genesis 4:6–7a)

4. *But if you do not do what is right, sin is* _____ *at your door; it desires to have you, but you must master it.* (Genesis 4:7b)

5. Jesus is saying, *When you hate Christians you hate* _____.

6. God gave Cain chances to choose the light, and He does the same for us.

   A. Choose _____.

   B. If you don't stay in the light, respond to the _____ of God.

   C. If you sin, _____ and _____.

1. Briefly share a memory of sibling rivalry from childhood. Have you outgrown rivalry with your siblings? Comment. (If you are an only child, think about rivalry with friends.)

   _____

   _____

2. What stood out to you in the video? Why?

   _____

Day 1

DARKNESS IS OUR NATURAL STATE

We each have a tendency to minimize our depravity. Though we know we aren't perfect, we tend to think we are pretty nice people. However, one glimpse of the holiness, of the pure light of God, exposes us for the frauds we are. Instead of "nice" women, we absolutely must be "new" women.

1. Read Isaiah 6:1–8.

   A. Describe what Isaiah saw in verses 1–4.

      _____

      _____

   B. Describe Isaiah's feelings and words as a result of this vision (verse 5). Why do you think he felt this way?

      _____

      _____

   C. What did the seraph do and say? What do you think was the significance of this?

      _____

      _____

   D. What evidence do you find that Isaiah was now ready for service (verse 8)?

      _____

      _____

   In the same way, the disciples had an early encounter with the Lord that revealed their sinfulness to them.

2. Read Luke 5:1–11.

    A. Describe the miracle and why it might have astonished the fishermen.

    _____

    _____

    B. What was Peter's response in Luke 5:8? Why, do you think?

    _____

    _____

    C. Who else is mentioned in verse 10?

    _____

    D. What two things does Jesus tell them in verse 10b? What similarities do you see to
    the passage in Isaiah?

    _____

    _____

"The Miraculous
Draught of Fishes"
Raphael (1483–1520)

    E. What insight does Raphael's painting give you into this incident?

    _____

    _____

3. Can you share a time when you were acutely aware of the holiness of God and how it
made you feel? Do you see any parallels with Isaiah or Simon Peter? If so, what?

_____

_____

4. Describe the scene John witnessed in Matthew 17:2.

_____

_____

It is with the characteristic of light that John begins his first letter. He was a firsthand witness to the glory of the Lord and so, with authority, he introduces the first principle that God is Light. John's letter has been compared to an exquisite piece of music—he starts with a theme and then builds on it. Observe how he does this.

5. What basic theme does John state in 1 John 1:5?

_____

6. On this basic theme John builds. Find the negative and positive corollaries.

A. Negative

1:6 _____

_____

2:9 _____

_____

B. Positive

1:7 _____

_____

2:10 _____

_____

Begin learning your memory passage.

Day 2

DO NOT BE LIKE CAIN

Memories of sibling rivalry in childhood are common, and often funny, for children are expected to act in childish ways. But if nothing is done to train the child in the right way, if nothing is done to "drive the folly" out of a child, the stories are no longer funny, but tragic. Without the transforming power of the Holy Spirit, we are all capable of the depravity of Cain. Each time we resist the light of God, the enemy has a victory, and a stronger hold on our lives. Sin is crouching at the door, longing to overpower us. History shows man is capable of great evil when he resists the light.

Cain's name has become synonymous with sin and darkness. He is the antithesis of the imprint of Christ—instead of reflecting Christ, he reflects the face of the evil one, who was given free reign in his heart. He was a liar and a murderer. Cain was not a believer, for John says he belonged to the evil one. But don't assume that because you are a believer, you are immune from being overpowered by sin. John's letter was written to believers, and he warns believers: "Do not be like Cain" (1 John 3:12a).

7. In 1 John 3:12, what are we told? Did Cain hate Abel because Abel was wicked? If not, why did Cain hate him?

_____

_____

The above point is key, for Cain is a prototype of the world, which hates Christians because their light exposes darkness, because their righteousness exposes sin. Christians are ridiculed, persecuted, and martyred, not because they are evil, but because they are good. John Stott explains:

> *It is not just hatred, but hatred of Christian people, which reveals the world in its true colours, for in their persecution of the Church, their antagonism to Christ is revealed.*[1]

8. What does Jesus say in John 15:18–19? (John repeats this in 1 John 3:13.)

_____

_____

9. What did Jesus say to Saul of Tarsus when he was riding to Damascus to persecute Christians (Acts 9:3–5)?

_____

_____

"Conversion of St. Paul"
Caravaggio (1573–1610)

10. With the above words of Jesus in mind, both to the disciples and to Paul, explain why it is so wrong, for us, as believers, to bear malice toward our brother in the Lord.

_____

_____

It is also true that as we love our brothers, we are loving Jesus. This is one of the keys to living in love with Jesus.

11. John tells us that you can tell who a person's father is (God or Satan) by one important attitude. What is it, according to 1 John 3:14–15?

_____

If someone claims to be a Christian yet has a hatred of Christian people, do not be deceived. He is not bearing the mark of a Christian, but the mark of Satan.

12. Read Genesis 4:1–5.

A. Who were the sons and what were their professions (vv. 1–2)?

_____

B. What clues can you find in verses 3–4 that Cain's offering was substandard and Abel's excellent?

_____

C. What was the Lord's response to each offering (vv. 4b–5a)?

_____

"The Bound Lamb"
Francisco de Zurbaran
(about 1598–1664)

13. Later in the Old Testament, God commands the sacrifice of a lamb without blemish as a foreshadowing of Jesus, the Perfect Lamb of God. What thoughts do you have as you meditate on the above painting, _The Bound Lamb_?

_____

_____

Many commentators feel that Cain's sin was *not* that he failed to bring a blood sacrifice, but his heart attitude. Abel brought the best that he could, an offering that cost him, and in so doing, happened upon a blood sacrifice. Cain's attitude was "I'll just bring whatever to get by," and so he brought "some fruits and vegetables."

14. Describe some actions that reveal a heart "just trying to get by," instead of one that is passionate about pleasing God.

_____

_____

15. Cain is now at a crossroads. The Lord comes to Cain and sheds light on the two paths before him. Describe each path and its consequences (Genesis 4:6–7).

_____

_____

_____

16. Describe a time in the last week when you experienced the conviction of the Holy Spirit, either by a *holy twist* or through the sword of the Spirit, which is the Word of God. What happened? How did you respond? (You don't have to share this in the group.)

_____

_____

17. Read Genesis 4:8–16.

    A. Note the number of times the word *brother* occurs in this passage. What point is being made, do you think?

    _____

    B. Why do you think God asks Cain where his brother is?

    _____

    C. How does Cain respond?

    _____

Charles Spurgeon reflects:

> If it had not been on record in the page of inspiration, we might almost have doubted whether a man could speak so impudently when actually conscious that God himself was addressing him. Men blaspheme frightfully, but it is usually because they forget God, and ignore his presence; but Cain was conscious that God was speaking to him. . . . To what a shameful pitch of presumptuous impudence had Cain arrived.[2]

D. What is Cain's punishment and why (vv. 10–12)?

_____

_____

E. What evidence of mercy do you see God still extending to Cain (vv. 13–16)?

_____

_____

"CAIN SLAYING ABEL"
PETER PAUL RUBENS (1577–1640)

18. What thoughts do you have as you meditate on the above painting by Rubens?

_____

_____

Day 3

FIRST CHANCE: CHOOSE TO STAY IN THE LIGHT

(Kathy) After I gave my life to Christ, I really had to change the template of how I processed right and wrong. If someone did me wrong, I wanted to do them wrong. If someone didn't like the way I was doing something, I thought, *Tough—that's your problem.* Now, because of the light of God exposing my darkness, all the rules have changed. My old rules looked nothing like God's rules.

Brick by brick, I had to start tearing down my fortress and then rebuild—this time God's fortress. I needed to use His blueprint, His bricks, and His boundaries. I'll give you an example from my early years as a Christian. The light of God made me respond entirely differently from the way I would have if I had been operating in the dark.

I couldn't wait to go to church on Sunday when I first understood that I could have a relationship with Jesus. I loved learning about Him through the sermons. I loved singing the new hymns. I loved reading my Bible. My mom quickly grew increasingly worried about my "newfound faith." She didn't understand the whole "born-again thing." It was a separate religion to her. Here I was, experiencing the greatest find of my life, and my mom was heartsick that I was "joining some cult" and "being led astray."

I couldn't help but continue to have a passion in my heart to know everything I could know about Jesus. I found that I had a growing desire to be baptized and to be immersed in water. I wanted to experience the whole thing—the beautiful symbol of dying to the old way of life and coming up a new creation: death, burial, and resurrection. I wanted to be baptized the way I think Jesus may have been. I started to go to Friday night classes and offered to sing a special song at the baptism. At this time in my life I was writing songs almost every day about Jesus and my love for Him. My mom continued to get upset. I knew she didn't understand.

Because my extended family was so close, and because my dad had died when I was fifteen, my mother shared her apprehensions about my choices with "the family." One night a couple of my uncles came over to talk to me. They never communicated that much with me, but now they had a lot to say:

"You're destroying your mother."

"Isn't our church good enough for you?"

"Your father's rolling over in his grave."

"Stick to your own religion."

I remained silent. Deep down I knew they were trying to "protect me." How could they possibly understand? When they left, I thought long and hard about the whole situation. Even then I had a sense that God was changing my heart. It would have been typical of me to think and to say, "Too bad. You're ignorant. You don't have a clue. I'm going to do what I want to do."

No person helped me sift through my thoughts. No person helped me with my decision. Just as 1 John 2:27 says, the Spirit of God alone shed light into my soul through His Word and through His peace. I knew that I loved God and I knew He loved me. I wanted so desperately to live for Him. Baptism is a way to identify with Christ and be obedient to His commandment. But I was sure of my salvation whether I got baptized or not. I also knew that God commanded me to honor my mother and father. If this was going to put a wedge between my mother and me, then I knew I should wait to get baptized. So I did. Staying in the light, in this situation, meant waiting to be baptized until my mom had a peace about it.

I did go to the baptismal service. I did sing a song. I remember being teary about not being able to join everyone else, but I had such a calm in my soul that I was doing the right thing. A couple of days later I knew that my family would be inquisitive about what happened. My mother told them that I ended up not getting baptized. One aunt said, "But how do you really know that Kathleen didn't get baptized?" That really hurt because I knew why I came to make the choice I made, and they thought I was being deceptive. I had to trust that God would defend me. Staying in the light in this situation meant keeping my mouth shut and allowing God to defend me to this aunt. (This aunt, by the way, was my Aunt Woolie, with whom God gave me the opportunity to pray, to receive Christ, when she was dying of cancer.)

I was able to make the choice I made because the Lord gave me the big picture. Sometimes He will do that if we really seek Him. Sometimes, especially as young believers, we can get a chip on our shoulder and think, *All of you are so spiritually ignorant. I'm just going to do what I need to do. I'm going to do what God told me to do.* Isn't it funny how often we blame God for the choices we make? We must be very careful when we say, "God said this to me or God told me to do this . . ." Most of the time this kind of talk is cloaked in our own agendas. I knew I had to wait and let my mother see the difference Jesus would make in my life. I thank God that I had the soberness of heart and that His Spirit gave me the fruit of patience and self-control to truly wait. God needed time to work in my mom's heart.

There is definitely a relationship between John's principle of walking in His light and walking in His love. God's light allowed me to see His path of love and to walk in it. And in time, He honored my obedience before my mother and my family.

I don't know exactly how this happened, but somehow, a number of years later, my mom got an "OK" from a Catholic priest. She got a written letter from him that I could be baptized. That is almost unheard of. Although my mother wasn't pleased with it, she gave me the choice. So I did get baptized. I really wanted my mom to come, but she didn't. Many women at the church rejoiced with me that night. They brought me precious little mementos because they knew it was a bittersweet experience.

When my mother got sick, her heart softened about many issues. She even apologized about some of the things we went through together. She understood more now. Facing death often has a way of helping us see what's important and what is not. Many realize then that it isn't about being in a particular denomination—it's about knowing Jesus. I'm thankful she finally saw that I was trying to be a better woman and do what God would want me to do.

If only I could make those choices all the time.

As we move through the day as believers, the highest road is always to simply stay in the light, to choose, as my friend Allyson puts it, "the next right thing." Cain could have done that by giving his best. We can do that too. That is always the first and highest choice.

Continue learning your memory passage.

19. The best possible life we can choose for ourselves is to stay in the light, to do the next right thing. God has given us several resources to show us the right path, the path of light. What are these resources, according to the following?

A. Romans 2:14–15 _____

_____

B. Psalm 119:105_____

_____

C. John 14:25–26 _____

_____

It is vital to realize that apart from God, we will not choose the right path. We need both His Spirit and His Word to choose the right path. Some of the darkest days on earth are recorded in the book of Judges. What was the reason for the depravity? "Every man did that which was right in his own eyes" (Judges 21:25b KJV).

In *The Divine Conspiracy*, Dallas Willard tells of a pilot practicing high-speed maneuvers in a fighter jet. She became disoriented. The controls told her she was going straight down, but her equilibrium told her she was headed up a steep ascent. She trusted herself and not the controls and flew straight into the ground.[3] If we do not trust the Word of God and instead trust in our own hearts, we too may fly straight into the ground.

20. Our consciences are our first defense against the enemy, but God has given the believer two other valuable resources, for our consciences can be seared. The Holy Spirit illumines the Word of God and brings it to our remembrance. Give an example of how the Word of God led you in a different direction than you might have gone had you trusted your own instincts.

_____

_____

(Kathy) Sometimes, because of all the fires I have created in my life by wrong choices, it is just enough for me that God says: "Because I said so."

21. What does Proverbs 14:12 teach? Can you think of some illustrations of this proverb?

_____

_____

22. How did God's Spirit and God's Word show Kathy the right path?

_____

23. What effect did Kathy's sensitivity to God have on her relationship with her family?

_____

(Dee) One of the things I find interesting about Kathy's story is that the disagreement was about one of those peripheral issues. Baptism *is very* important, but it is not a central truth—it doesn't have to do with who Jesus is, or how we are saved. There are also those who could build a strong case for Jesus' having been sprinkled instead of immersed. There are those who could build a strong case for the beauty of infant baptism as a means of dedication, as well as for a believer's baptism. Remember Francis Schaeffer's point that divisions between believers usually occur not because of a difference in doctrine, but because of "a lack of love, and the bitter things that are said by true Christians in the midst of differences."[4]

24. Are there some peripheral issues on which you disagree with Christians with whom you frequently interact? How do you believe God would have you handle this in order to stay in the light?

_____

_____

25. In your life today, what would it look like if you stayed in the light?

_____

_____

Finish learning your memory passage.

Day 4

SECOND CHANCE: RESPOND TO THE CONVICTION OF GOD

When the Lord looked with favor on Abel and his offering, but not on Cain and his offering, anger and depression welled up in Cain.

So Cain was very angry, and his face was downcast. (Genesis 4:5b)

Isn't that like most of us? God asks us to do something, and we don't; then when we suffer a consequence, we get angry with Him. We can even get into a funk about it. Though sin is not the only cause for depression, it is one possible cause. So it is always wise to ask yourself, when you're down, if there is a particular sin in your life that is keeping out the joy and light of God.

Cain had disobeyed God, and now he was disheartened. Even though he had chosen his own way, God cared about his pain. When you are suffering because of bad choices, God doesn't condemn you, saying: Well, kiddo, you deserve it. You made your bed, now lie in it. No. God cares for you. He comes to you and entreats you. The smartest thing in the world you can do at that point is swallow your pride and yield to the Spirit.

This is so significant: God gives Cain a choice.

> *Why is your face so dark with rage? It can be bright with joy if you will do what you should! But if you refuse to obey, watch out. Sin is waiting to attack you, longing to destroy you. But you can conquer it!* (Genesis 4:6b–7 TLB)

26. Review the two choices before Cain and the consequences of each.

_____

_____

(Dee) We have a choice. And that choice either will open the door to the Spirit flowing in, flooding our hearts with light and love, or it will open the door to the evil one, flooding our hearts with darkness, depression, and despair. The New International Version (NIV) says, "Sin is crouching at your door; it desires to have you . . ."

27. Think about times when this choice lay before you.

A. Share what you remember about a recent time when you did not respond to the Spirit of God and chose the wrong path. What were the consequences? Why, do you think, you failed to respond—and what can you learn?

_____

_____

B. Share what you remember about what happened in your life when you did respond to the Spirit of God and chose to obey.

_____

_____

28. Right now, is there a situation in your life in which these two choices lay before you? What is it? What will you choose and how?

_____

_____

29. From Psalm 32:3–4, describe how David felt when he kept silent about his sin.

_____

_____

(*Dee*) After Steve and I had three children, God gave us the desire to adopt from overseas orphanages. The first daughter we adopted was Annie, a precious five-year-old from an orphanage in Seoul. Our eleven-year-old daughter, Sally, was thrilled that she was going to finally have a sister—that is, until the day Annie arrived. Sally became very jealous of her sister, and it escalated into a much more serious situation than simple childhood rivalry. Sally tells of how it began.

I had been the baby of the family for twelve years, and the only girl, and the center of attention.

I was excited to have a sister. I was excited to have somebody to play with. But as soon as this adorable little doll with shiny black hair walked off the plane, I suddenly felt huge—I was in my chubby adolescent phase. I had braces; I was nothing compared to this little beauty. I saw all the attention suddenly shift from me to her.

This isn't good, I thought to myself.

My heart began to change. I let envy take hold of me. I became jealous, depressed, and sad. I really didn't love my new sister, and I was very angry with her. She bugged me. I didn't want to talk to her. I didn't want to be with her. Misery was my state of heart for four or five months.

During this time we became very concerned for Sally. She stopped eating, sleeping, and wanting to be with people. Steve and I began to pray in earnest for her. One night we saw God begin to intervene when we went to a Christian concert as a family. Sally remembers the night vividly.

After the concert, one of the singers stepped forward. He talked about Jesus and His love for us. He said, "When you feel like you've got a sin that's controlling your life, give it to the Lord. Tell Him you're wrong, ask for forgiveness, and He'll cleanse you from it. He has the power to change you."

I knew there was this "yuck" in my life, this gross stuff, this envy, this jealousy, this sadness. I seemed powerless to get rid of it, and I didn't know what to do. I was so frustrated. I knew it was wrong, but I didn't know how to love my sister. So I just said, "God, I just need You to change me. I need You to take this from me. I'm so sorry. You know I can't do this. I can't love her. I can't get rid of this jealousy. I'm so mad at her. Just take this away, please, and give me some of Your love to give to her."

You know what? That was the turning point for me. God began to change my perception of my sister. I went home, and it was as if God had given me new eyes for my sister. She was no longer a competitor for my parents' love.

I began to see that my parents loved me, too, just as much. And I began to see her as a hurting child who not only desperately needed the love of my parents, but she also needed the love of her sister.

God gave me a love for her that was definitely not my own. Since then things have just gotten so much better. The following year we really became close. It was a slow process, and sometimes I did struggle with envy, but the Lord really did change my heart.

We could see a definite change in Sally's attitude, but Sally was still struggling with sleeplessness and irritability. Because her dad is acquainted with clinical depression, not just as a physician but personally, he realized she might be experiencing a clinical depression, brought on by a chemical imbalance. (Those born with a chemical imbalance may not experience depression until they have their first major stress, and then the symptoms of the imbalance become recognizable.) I love it when Kathy tells women that "Prozac" is not a dirty word. She says, and I cheer, "Good for you for getting help." Depression is complicated, and often there is not just one simple solution. There are so many Christians who unintentionally heap shame and guilt on their depressed brothers and sisters, telling them that antidepressants are wrong, and that they should simply trust God. Would they tell a diabetic to forgo his insulin and trust God? Jesus said, "The sick need a physician," so we went to a physician.

In recent years, studies have found that people who have a chemical imbalance of some kind, leading to a clinical depression or a mental illness, and who do not get medical help, can suffer permanent damage to their brains. It has also been discovered that it can be detrimental to go off and on medication when there is a genuine imbalance. Each time the individual goes back on, his antidepressant is less effective. Oh, the pain we can inflict on others, when we, in our arrogance, give advice on matters about which we are uninformed.

When Sally went forward at that Christian concert, she had a heart change toward her sister. Now, with medicine for her chemical imbalance, her body began to heal as well. She was eating again, sleeping again. Sally continues:

> Annie and I spent six years together before I went to college. The night before I was to leave, she climbed up on my top bunk and got under the covers with me. I was just holding her, and we prayed a little together, and then she looked at me. With tears in her eyes, she said, "You know what, Sally?"
>
> I said, "What, Annie?"
>
> "You're my very best friend."
>
> I said, "God, thank You. Thank You for being faithful for changing my heart and giving me a love that I didn't have on my own. Thank You for healing me and my relationship with my sister."

In the opening to John's letter, he tells us that following the principles in his letter will cause us to experience:

A. fellowship with God

B. fellowship with one another

C. fullness of joy

30. How did Cain lose all of these things? How did Sally Brestin lose these things? What was the key to restoration?

_____

_____

31. What stood out to you from Sally's story? Is there an application for you?

_____

_____

_____

Day 5

THIRD CHANCE: REPENT OF YOUR SIN

The amazing truth is that even after Cain had murdered his brother, God was offering yet again an opportunity for forgiveness. When He asked Cain, "Where is your brother?" it was not because God did not know! He was giving Cain another chance—a chance to confess and repent of the murder of his brother.

God surely hates the shedding of innocent blood. But He would have forgiven Cain even that, if Cain had confessed and repented. There is only one sin that is outside the grace of God, and that is the rejection of Jesus Christ, because when we reject Christ, we reject our only lifeline. John addresses *this* sin, which Jesus called "blasphemy against the Holy Spirit" (which does not mean swearing, but rejecting the lifeline God has provided) or, as John puts it, "the sin that leads to death."

32. Read 1 John 5:16–17 carefully. What does John say to do for the brother who is not sinning the "sin that leads to death" (v. 16a)? What about the brother who *is* sinning the "sin that leads to death" (v. 16b)?

_____

This is a difficult passage, but you will see, as you continue to study this letter, that John is continually making a contrast between a genuine brother and a counterfeit brother. John Stott says that in context of the whole letter, "the sin that leads to death" is the rejection of Christ. There are those who *claim* to be Christians, but in reality they have rejected Christ. They *look* like "brothers and sisters," but when Jesus returns, they will be like the five foolish virgins, like the counterfeit believers of whom Jesus will say, "I never knew you." We cannot pray for them to be saved apart from Christ, for that is a prayer God will not hear. However, we can and should pray for brothers and sisters who have sinned in other ways. For other than the rejection of Christ, there is absolutely no sin, no matter how grievous, that is outside God's grace.

Spend some time in intercession for your loved ones, in their fight against sin. Pray through 1 John 1:6–9 for your children, or for a few dear friends.

33. Read Isaiah 1:15–21.

A. What sin on the part of the Israelites had grieved the heart of God? (See particularly verses 15 and 21.)

_____

B. Yet what glorious promise does God give even to murderers, whose hands "are full of blood," according to Isaiah 1:15?

_____

34. One of the ways Satan keeps Christians defeated is by causing them to doubt the power of God to completely cleanse our sins. God has told us to use the sword of the Spirit, which is the Word of God, to defeat our enemy. Find a word or a phrase in each of the following verses to defeat the enemy.

   A. 1 John 1:9_____

   B. 1 John 2:1–2_____

   C. 1 John 2:12_____

   D. 1 John 5:11–12_____

Is there a sin in your past that is *still* causing you guilt? Jesus died to pay for that sin. Don't hold on to it. Give it to Jesus—believe His promises—otherwise, you are saying that His death was not sufficient to pay for your sin.

The only unforgivable sin is the rejection of Christ. But there is no other sin, no matter how heinous, that Christ's blood cannot cleanse. We've seen many women lock themselves in self-imposed prisons of guilt over abortion when God longs to forgive them. Though the shedding of innocent blood grieves God, a broken and contrite heart He will not despise. To think that Christ's blood is insufficient to cleanse from a sin, no matter what it is, is to minimize His sacrifice. Yet we've seen this happen again and again. Women carry the stain of abortion on their hands and the burden on their hearts. Just as when God asked Cain a question so that He could get to the truth, God longs for women to be set free from the chains they've held themselves in by acknowledging the truth.

Women might say to God, "What about my baby? What about what I did?"

And God says, "What about your baby? I have your baby. I want a relationship with you."

He never condemns us, but gives us a chance to confess, repent, and be set free of shame and guilt. He always wants to get to the truth, because the truth will set us free. Then He will fully forgive, fully cleanse.

Because so many women who have had abortions cannot believe in a love so great, in a grace so far-reaching, they carry their burden of guilt, and it affects not only them, but also their attitude toward their husbands, toward their children, and toward their world. We have seen the power of God released in women who finally can trust in His forgiveness.

(Kathy) I experienced this when I was in Turkey doing a conference for military wives. I had already sung for about an hour and a half, and the women asked me to sing some more. Because they were in no hurry to leave, I decided to sing "A Baby's Prayer." Statistics tell us that one out of every four women have had an abortion. I knew there had to be some of them there. So I said,

> *Some of you have suffered a great deal with guilt and shame from the choice of abortion. This song is for you.*

Many women cried that night, confessing abortions and other sins. The prison doors were being flung open and they were being set free. The next morning, as I was preparing to sing a couple of songs, a woman came up to me and grabbed my hand. She spoke to me through teary eyes:

Kathy, I had an abortion twenty-five years ago. I've never told a soul. I want you to know that I slept through the night last night for the first time in twenty-five years. I feel free. I feel at peace. Thank you for allowing me to experience God's forgiveness.

I often tell women:

You can't "out-sin" the love of God. He's not going to appear to you one day and say, "I've had it. You really did it this time. That's it. I'm done." If that were true, His dying on the cross would all be in vain. Because we calculate things and see things through the eyes of our human nature, we think there is going to be an end to His love.

We think that the Forgiveness River is going to run dry because we've dipped in it one too many times. I know, I've been there. But He says, "It will never happen." Please, don't ever give up on God and how much He loves you. And don't give up on yourself—because that is when death will have free reign in you. That is when the enemy will have a heyday. He wants to win.

Until you close your eyes for that last time on earth, there is always hope. So always take the opportunity to say, "Lord, I give this to You once again."

It's like the thief on the cross. When he humbled himself and acknowledged the Savior of the World, God said to him, "Today you will be with Me in paradise." Yes, today God hears you, wherever you've been, whatever you've done. He'll say,

Take My hand. We're going to conquer this thing together.

35. What have you learned this week that stood out to you? How will you apply it to your life?

_____

_____

PRAYER TIME

Cluster in small groups. Look at your answer to the last question. Be willing to lift it up and allow the women to pray for you.

If you know the following chorus, you may wish to close your prayer time with it:

Grace, grace, God's grace
Grace that will pardon and cleanse within;
Grace, grace, God's grace
Grace that is greater than all our sin!
(Public Domain)

WALKING IN THE LIGHT

One of John's primary themes is the contrast between the genuine and the counterfeit. If we want to experience the presence, power, and peace of God, we must learn to walk in genuine repentance. So often we'll stay stuck, and instead of growing in holiness, we keep walking in the same rut and wondering, "Where is the victory?"

Without even realizing it, we may have deceived ourselves, walking in "counterfeit repentance." It *looks* like genuine repentance in many ways, but because there is no fruit, we know it is not the real thing. There is no power in counterfeit repentance. Women have told us that this lesson is one that has changed their lives, has gotten them "unstuck," and has taken them to the high places. We pray this will happen for you. Do it with diligence, asking God to illumine your thoughts and to give you the strength to walk in *genuine* repentance, to walk in the light.

VIDEO NOTES FOR WEEK 5
WALKING IN THE LIGHT

Thoughts I want to remember:

Repentance requires change.

1. In *Falling in Love with Jesus*, we mentioned three states of spiritual growth:

   Children

   Fathers

   Young man

2. John addresses these three groups of people in 1 John 2:12–14b, and tells them the mighty power of God is in them.

   A. Children (First Love)

   I write to you, dear children, because your sins have been _forgiven_ *on account of his name.* (I John 2:12)

B. Fathers (Invincible Love)

I write to you, fathers, because you have known him who is from the ___beginning___.
(1 John 2:13a)

C. Young Men (Wilderness Love)

I write to you, young men, because you are strong, and the ___Word___ *of*
___God___ *lives in you, and you have overcome the evil one.* (1 John 2:14b)

3. What did Jesus say to the man at the healing pool?

Pick up your ___mat___ ___and___ ___walk___!

4. Three kinds of counterfeit repentance:

A. ___Gut-wrenching emotion w/out behavior change___

Example: ___men who cast out their wives +___
___then made sacrifices which God didn't accept___

because God was upset because the men had broken the marriage vow.

B. ___Sorry about the consequences but not broken before God.___

Example: ___King Saul asked David to come play harp to soothe___
___his soul. But Saul was jealous of David + threw___

spears at him.

C. ___Partial or delayed   u turn in behavior___

Example: ___God to Saul: wipe out all Amalachites.___
___Saul wiped out just some of Amalachites.___
___To obey is better than to sacrifice.___

ICEBREAKER *(Hear from as many women as are willing to share.)*

1. Which kind of counterfeit repentance have you practiced most frequently? Give an example.
___gut wrenching emotion w/out behavior change.___

2. What stood out to you in the video and why?
___Holding onto sinful behaviors is not God.___

"against you Lord + only you have I sinned."

God can" — God can. Put in prayers in the can.

Zondervan The Bible Experience with African American actors.

UNDERSTANDING AND OVERCOMING THE DECEIT OF OUR HEARTS

Although God's desire is for us to be His and to be holy, He also knows that we will fail. In fact, John tells us that if we claim we can always walk in the light, we "live in a world of illusion," deceiving ourselves. Jeremiah tells us our hearts are deceitful. Until we understand the depravity and deceitfulness of our own hearts, we will not understand how desperately we need to continually come before the searching light of God—allowing Him to shed light on our darkness through His Word and through His Spirit. We will also try to live in love with Jesus in our own strength instead of in His.

The passages you will look at today have to do with how we are deceived, but also tell us the secrets to overcoming that deceit. One of the most powerful tools we have for victory is God's Word, but we must hide it in our hearts. If you have been lazy about doing your homework or about the memory passages, determine, at this halfway point, to make a genuine U-turn. Don't do it in your own strength, but rest in God's grace to empower you. If you have already been doing this successfully, *continue* walking in His grace. The psalmist writes:

> *Keep me from deceitful ways;*
> *be gracious to me through your law.*
> *I have chosen the way of truth;*
> *I have set my heart on your laws.*
> *I hold fast to your statutes, O LORD;*
> *do not let me be put to shame.*
> (Psalm 119:29–31)

Set your heart on this week's memory passage. Often, learning it a word at a time will best help you retain it.

1. Read 1 John 1:6–10 carefully again, and look for the five "If we" phrases. What is the behavior described in each verse, and what is the consequence for that behavior?

   A. 1:6: "If we" _____

   the consequence will be:_____

   B. 1:7: "If we" _____

   the consequence will be:_____

   C. 1:8: "If we" _____

   the consequence will be:_____

D. 1:9: "If we" _____

the consequence will be: _____

E. 1:10: "If we" _____

the consequence will be: _____

(Kathy) When a Christian is filled with grumbling, hate, and critical comments toward others, I often think, *What do they do when the door is closed and they talk to Jesus? Are they aware of their capacity to sin? Are they aware of the darkness in their hearts?* If you really talk to God about your behavior, I don't think you can have that kind of an attitude toward someone—at least not for long. You will always be convicted to show mercy, no matter someone's sin, if you are honest with God about yourself. If you stay in a state of continual repentance for your own sins, you will be merciful toward others. Repentance allows God's light to reveal your pride. He will show you your sin. Then the mercy you receive from the Lord for yourself can be given to others. When I find myself getting critical, I usually tell myself:

> *Troccoli, you need a spiritual shower.*

(Dee) Seeing the speck in your sister's eye, but ignoring the log in your own, is one evidence of a failure to come before the searching light of God. There are certain areas where the church has sadly lacked compassion, where we have failed to love our brothers and sisters. For example, so often the church has failed to give true understanding and support to the innocent victim of divorce. How often we have prayed and wept with a woman who did not want the divorce, but her husband had another woman, or didn't want to live with a Christian, and abandoned and divorced her. Yet *she* is made to feel like an outcast in the church. Likewise, Kathy has seen how often Christians ask a woman not to have an abortion, but then shame her if she gives her baby up for adoption. What are we thinking? We can almost hear John, the "Son of Thunder" as Jesus nicknamed him, looking down from heaven and roaring: "How can the love of God be in you?"

We are also prone to judge in an area where we have *never* struggled—whether it is with obesity, substance abuse, stealing, rebellious children, or marital problems. Next week we will look at the story of a woman who was caught in the chains of homosexuality, but has been delivered. She has seen, firsthand, how poorly the church responds to those struggling to overcome in *this* area.

We tend to be compassionate only in the areas where we have had battles. We judge people from our own life experiences. But that's not the love of Jesus. When I was speaking in a woman's prison in Omaha recently, my dear friend Eunice, who is working with the female inmates said: "Dee, behind every one of these women is a story that would break your heart. I truly believe that if I had suffered what they had, I would have ended up behind bars as well." I admired her statement because she is being honest with the depravity of her own heart. If we think, *I would never raise a child who would become a drug addict; or I would never be so foolish as to marry the kind of man who would abandon me; or I would never be tempted to have an abortion;* or *I would never let my weight get that out of control*—then the pride of our hearts has deceived us.

2. Read 1 Corinthians 10:1–13.

   A. What happened to the Israelites who had been delivered out of slavery (v. 5)?

   _____

   B. Why does the Lord write to us about them (v. 6)?

   _____

   C. What were some of the sins that grieved the Lord (vv. 7–10)?

   _____

   D. What warning does God repeat (vv. 11–12)?

   _____

   E. If you think you are beyond temptation in an area, how does this passage shed light on the deceitfulness of your heart?

   _____

3. What other clear signs does John give in 1 John 2 that point to a heart that has been deceived?

   A. 1 John 2:4_____

   B. 1 John 2:9_____

   C. 1 John 2:15_____

We will look more carefully at this last verse next week, but for now, be aware that the transitory things of this world are one of the main traps of the enemy. Jesus warned of "the deceitfulness of wealth" (Matthew 13:22) choking out fruitfulness from our lives. John pleads with us to keep ourselves from idols (1 John 5:21). We must be diligent to keep the Lord first in our lives. A clear sign that someone has been deceived and has moved into the shadows is an obsession with the things that will pass away.

4. Read James 1:22–27.

   A. In verse 22, what kind of behavior is deceitful to ourselves?

   _____

B. In verses 23–25, what word picture is given to describe the person who deceives himself? What picture and promise are given of genuine repentance?

_____

_____

C. Find three clear signs of someone who is walking in genuine repentance in verses 26–27. What similarities do you see to the letter of John?

_____

_____

_____

_____

(*Dee*) I am blessed to be in a particularly healthy church. Many in my church have been role models for me because of their radically obedient and loving lives. We also are blessed with very strong biblical preaching, and pastors and elders who walk humbly before God. Our senior pastor, Mike Lano, once gave a sermon on *counterfeit* repentance, listing three common forms. Isn't it amazing that we can counterfeit even repentance? Yet I realized that I have done them *all*. Recognizing the forms has helped me to walk more consistently in genuine repentance. I love it in the light! That's where I experience the presence of God, real intimacy with other believers, and a fullness of joy—just as John promised. We'll begin our study of counterfeit repentance tomorrow.

Day 2

COUNTERFEIT # 1: EMOTIONAL REPENTANCE WITHOUT A U-TURN

(*Dee*) One of my favorite people is Bible teacher Jan Silvious. She is *so* real, down-to-earth, and wise. When she counsels people who call in to her radio broadcast, she cuts right to the heart of the problem, like an expert surgeon. She has helped thousands of women to "get well." My husband describes her counsel as a triple dose of common sense.

Jan is continually urging all of us to be "big girl Christians" instead of "little girl Christians." Once, when I was speaking with Jan at a women's event, there was an altar call, and many women came forward. Some stayed up there a long time, sobbing. Afterward, Jan and I took a walk outside. It was a balmy summer night in the Smoky Mountains, and as we walked along the quaint little streets of Gatlinburg, I was eager to hear her thoughts about all that had transpired that night. She told me about a friend who once asked her, "What's your favorite bad feeling?"

Then Jan said, "Ever since that time I have learned to ask that question when I see emotional responses."

I realized what Jan was saying was that many of us, particularly as women, like to *feel* things and hold on to them. Somehow it makes us feel more alive. Of course, emotion in itself is not bad, it's just that we can "camp around feelings" that cause destruction. We can settle into self-pity, anger, guilt, and all sorts of webs. That's why, especially as women, we may weep before God but do nothing about our self-made prisons. They have become comfortable for us.

Right now our youngest child, Annie, who is nineteen, is with Youth with a Mission. During Thanksgiving break, she told me:

> *Mom, I used to go to the altar weeping, but then I didn't do anything about it. Now I am going to the altar and not weeping, and I am doing something about it.*

Jan Silvious has experienced the frustration, as a counselor, of seeing the tears but no behavioral change. She has heard, as I have, people plead with God, saying:

> *I only want Your will, Lord.*

> *Let me be the woman You want me to be.*

The problem is that those are empty prayers when one doesn't obey even the simple things that God has *already* revealed to them.

Many of us *think* we have repented because of the gut-wrenching emotion involved. But have we truly repented? In a couple of days or weeks or months, we begin questioning God.

> *Why haven't things changed?*

> *Why do I feel so defeated?*

One of the reasons we may be confused is that we are still going to church, still going to Bible study, and still going through the motions. We may feel sadness over our lack of closeness to God and our defeated lives.

The book of Malachi describes believers like this. These Israelites were not "big" sinners who worshiped idols or engaged in child sacrifice. They were the descendants of those who had returned to Jerusalem and had rebuilt the temple. But now they are just going through the motions. Their own hearts have deceived them because they think:

> *I'm bringing sacrifices to God.*

> *I'm weeping at the altar.*

> *But He doesn't answer my prayers!*

> *Doesn't He love me?*

Malachi clearly addresses one kind of counterfeit repentance. I have used this particular passage many times to bring comfort to women who have been dealt with treacherously by a husband. So often a woman will come to me and ask: "Why didn't God stop my husband from being unfaithful to me?" Or, "Why didn't He stop my husband from leaving me and the kids?" I sit down with them and walk them through the second chapter of Malachi. They leave with hope. They can see and perhaps feel that even though their husbands left them, God has seen their pain, is angry with the one who was treacherous with them, and will, Himself, never leave them or forsake them.

You may wish to prepare your heart for today's study by singing or praying this praise chorus:

Breathe on me, Breath of God, fill me with life anew
That I may love what Thou dost love and do what Thou wouldst do

Breathe on me, Breath of God, till I am wholly Thine,
Till all this earthly part of me glows with Thy fire divine.
(Public Domain)

5. Read Malachi 1:1 through 2:12 for the context:

   A. In Malachi 1:6, what questions are asked of the priests by the Lord?

   _____

   B. In Malachi 1:6–8, what behavior reveals their lack of devotion? What similarities did their offering have to Cain's offering?

   _____

   _____

   C. What evidence do you find in Malachi 1:7 that these men simply were not comprehending their sin?

   _____

   D. How does God describe their hearts in Malachi 2:1?

   _____

   _____

   E. The most prevalent explanation of Malachi 2:11–12 is that the men have cast aside their wives in order to marry foreign wives. What does Malachi say about this?

   _____

   _____

F. For what reason is God grieved other than that the men have cast aside their believing wives to marry pagan wives (v. 15)?

_____

_____

Scripture is clear that as a man learns to love his wife sacrificially, he becomes a picture of Jesus Christ (Ephesians 5:25–28). God's plan is for a man to cover his wife with protection and provision. When Ruth went to Boaz and asked him to "cover her," she was asking him to take care of her in the way God ordained for husbands (Ruth 3:9). The men in Malachi, instead of covering their wives with protection and provision, have "covered their wives with violence," casting them out on the streets. Not only have these men abandoned their responsibilities to the wives of their youth, they have not even had the mercy to give their wives certificates of divorce, freeing them to remarry. A woman in biblical days was destitute without a man's care.

When a woman comes to me who has endured a husband's treachery, I tell her, "God is angry with your husband, so you can let your anger go. He _will_ deal with him. Look at how God thundered at the men of Malachi."

6. Read Malachi 2:13–17.

A. Describe the emotion of the men at the altar (v. 13).

_____

B. What question did the men have, and what was the Lord's answer (vv. 14–15)?

_____

_____

C. In genuine repentance, you may have emotion, but what else is needed?

_____

So often the phrase "I hate divorce" is taken out of context from this passage in Malachi. God _does_ hate divorce, for it was never His intention for a family to be torn apart. Yet what He is saying here is that He hates the treachery that leads a man (or a woman) to "break faith" with the spouse of his youth, casting her aside for someone else. God's intention from the beginning was for a husband and wife to be one for life. God is _angry_ with the men who have cast their wives aside. He is irate that they are coming to the altar, weeping and wailing, but have done _nothing_ about their sin.

God also has a heart of mercy toward the victim—and I long for those who have been abandoned and abused to see this. God _does_ release the spouse who has been treated so treacherously. The phrase in 1 Corinthians, "not bound," is the strongest possible term describing freedom. If the unbeliever wants to go (and faithlessness reveals his true heart of unbelief), God says, "Let him do so. A believing man or woman is not bound in such circumstances" (1 Corinthians 7:15). Though the unfaithful spouse may not have bothered to give his partner a certificate of divorce, God frees the *victim* to divorce, setting him or her free to remarry. That is the mercy of God toward the victim. It was never His plan for her to be cast aside, but if she is, by a faithless spouse, He frees her.

My heart is grieved by the irony of the fact that so often the church is judgmental toward the innocent victim. Some people react in the following way and twist this passage: They take the "God hates divorce" statement out of context and shake their finger at the *victim*, when that is the opposite of how God intended this passage to be understood. The passage is a rebuke to the *perpetrator*, and it is meant to give compassion to the victim.

Does this mean God does not have mercy toward the one who did the treachery? God will always forgive, though there will be consequences for generations to come. Though God was wearied by the *counterfeit* repentance, He *would* have forgiven these men had they *truly* repented (see Malachi 4:2). I have a dear friend who confesses:

> *I left my husband because I decided I didn't want to be married to a farmer. It bothered me that he had dirt under his fingernails. I absolutely brought destruction to this fine man, and to our children. We both remarried, so I cannot "undo" what I did. But I have done a U-turn in my heart. I have confessed to God, to my ex-husband, and to our children that I was absolutely wrong. The painful consequences go on and on, not only for us, but for our children and, now, for our grandchildren. But in my brokenness I found Jesus. He has been absolutely merciful to me and has forgiven me. Though my sin was treacherous, He has covered me, cleansed me, and made me as white as snow.*

7. The men of Malachi did not truly repent but justified their unfaithfulness. What did the Lord tell them in Malachi 2:17?

_____

8. Summarize what have you learned from Malachi 2:13–16.

_____

_____

9. If you are married, are you being faithful, not only sexually, but also spiritually and emotionally, to your spouse and to the covenant you made before God? If not, what would true repentance look like?

_____

_____

10. How can you show a heart of compassion, as God does, to victims of divorce?

_____

11. Can you think of times when you have felt great emotion but have not changed your behavior? Has your emotion deceived you into *thinking* you repented?

_____

_____

12. Read Malachi 4:2 and find the promise and the condition for the promise.

_____

Day 3

COUNTERFEIT # 2: SORRY ABOUT CONSEQUENCES BUT NOT BROKEN BEFORE GOD

We can engage in alcohol abuse, sexual immorality, and harsh words and be sorry for the consequences. We see the toll taken on our bodies. We see the devastation these things can cause family and friends. Because we want to save our own skins, we turn for a time, *but unless we are repentant toward God, our own strength will always give out.* There's no true turning away from the sin and so no true power from the Holy Spirit for lasting change.

King Saul and King David give a clear contrast here.

13. Read 1 Samuel 17:55 through 18:9 and find as many reasons as you can for Saul's jealousy toward David.

_____

_____

In 1 Samuel 18:10, we are told "an evil spirit" from the Lord came forcefully upon Saul. Scripture consistently says that if you continue to resist God, He will allow your heart to harden. He will "turn you over to yourself." (See Romans 1:21–28 and Proverbs 1:22–33.) God may even allow a spirit from Satan to overcome you.

> . . . We must remember that God is also Lord of the spirits, and of the entire creation. He permits Satan to do certain things in the accomplishment of God's plan and purposes. . . . We must remember that God can use even the Devil and the evil spirits to carry out His designs and His plans. The expression, therefore, "an evil spirit from the Lord" does not mean that this spirit came directly from the Lord, but rather that He permitted it, and ordered it so that he was allowed to come and appear to the wicked King Saul.[1]
>
> (Dr. M. R. DeHaan)

14. In 1 Samuel 18:12, find the painful consequence that resulted from Saul's sin.

_____

15. Read 1 Samuel 18:28–29 and find how the consequences for Saul worsened. What evidence do you see that Saul's repentance was not genuine?

_____

_____

16. Read 1 Samuel 19:1–20:2.

   A. How did Jonathan show true friendship to David (19:4–5)?

   _____

   B. How did Saul's words *sound* like true repentance (19:6)?

   _____

   C. How did Saul's initial behavior look promising (19:7)?

   _____

   D. What evidence do you find for an unrepentant heart in Saul (19:8–10)?

   _____

   E. How is Saul an illustration of the truth John proclaims in 1 John 3:15 and
      1 John 4:7–8?

   _____

   _____

   F. God can see the heart, but often *we* are deceived by counterfeit repentance. How
      was Jonathan deceived (1 Samuel 20:1–2)?

   _____

   G. David then suggested a test to see if Saul would bear the fruit of genuine repentance.
      What was Jonathan's response (1 Samuel 20:4)? How did Jonathan feel when Saul
      failed the test (1 Samuel 20:34)?

   _____

   H. Why is it wise to look for fruit in the life of someone who has had a pattern of
      betrayal?

   _____

Being sorry about the consequences of your sin but not broken before God can look like true repentance. But in time, our own strength always gives out. Unless we are broken before God, God's presence will depart from us, as it did from Saul. We are still His children, but He cannot be with us if we remain in the dark.

17. What are some sinful behaviors that have costly consequences? What are some in your life?

_____

_____

18. Share a time when you were sorry about the consequences but not broken before God. Also tell what happened as a result.

_____

King David, in contrast to King Saul, was truly broken before God when confronted with his sin of adultery and murder.

19. Read 2 Samuel 12:13–25.

A. How did David respond when Nathan confronted him with his sin (2 Samuel 12:13)?

_____

B. What was David's prayer (2 Samuel 12:16–17)?

_____

C. Did God spare him (12:18)? How did the servants think David might respond?

_____

_____

D. How *did* David respond when he realized God had not spared him the consequences of his sin? How does this show David's repentance was genuine and not counterfeit (12:19–20)?

_____

_____

E. What did David believe about God and his baby that brought him comfort even in the midst of his sorrow (12:23)?

_____

F. How did God show mercy to David and Bathsheba despite their sin (12:24–25)?

_____

20. In the famous penitential Psalm 51, written after David's adultery with Bathsheba, what does David say in verse 4?

_____

That phrase has confused some, for surely David sinned against others when he committed adultery and murder. What godly men and women have come to see in this verse is that it isn't that David doesn't realize his sin toward man, but that God now looms above him as so awesome and holy that he can see no one else. He must first get right with God, the ultimate authority over his life. In *My Utmost for His Highest,* Oswald Chambers writes:

> *Very few of us know anything about conviction of sin. We know the experience of being disturbed because we have done wrong things. But conviction of sin by the Holy Spirit blots out every relationship on earth and makes us aware of only one—"Against You, You only, have I sinned."*[2]

David felt sorrow over the consequences of his sin, but his greatest heartbreak was over grieving God. This is true repentance. Does this mean we have to be brokenhearted every time we fail in our daily lives—every time we are irritable with someone, or rude, or forgetful of someone's needs? Though you will not always have the same sense of grief, you should always be aware that you have indeed grieved or offended God by hurting someone else. Your repentance, to be true, must be toward Him, as well as toward the one you have hurt.

Review your memory passage.

Day 4

COUNTERFEIT # 3: A PARTIAL TURN OR A DELAYED U-TURN

When you are truly sorry toward God, you are willing to give up the sin He shows you and to do whatever He tells you to do to make things right. Again, Saul exemplifies the counterfeit. When God told him to wipe out *all* the Amalekites, Saul partially obeyed, keeping the king and the best of the livestock alive.

We have such deceitful hearts. We often resort to our own rationale. This results in partial obedience. We repent of some of what God has convicted us of, but we still keep the sin close by so that we can have access to it when we desire it. We avoid the full U-turn because we rationalize that we aren't in full-fledged sin. We want partial credit for partial repentance. We will always come out looking good if we compare ourselves to Jack the Ripper, but if we compare ourselves to Jesus Christ, we will hang our heads low.

21. Read 1 Samuel 15:1–23.

A. What did God ask Saul to do (1 Samuel 15:3)?

_____

Later, when we look at the story of Esther, it is interesting to note that Haman, the one who was nearly successful in the holocaust against the Jews, was a descendant of the Amalekites. If Saul had obeyed, Haman would never have been born.

B. How did Saul *partially* obey (1 Samuel 15:8–9)?

_____

C. How is Saul oblivious to his disobedience (1 Samuel 15:13)?

_____

D. What humor do you see in Samuel's response (1 Samuel 15:14)?

_____

E. How does Saul still not comprehend (1 Samuel 15:18–21)?

_____

F. What were the consequences of this counterfeit repentance (1 Samuel 15:23)?

_____

All through his life Saul tried to gain the blessings of God without doing a genuine U-turn.

22. Read 1 Samuel 28:3–19.

A. According to 1 Samuel 28:3, what had happened to Samuel? What had happened to the mediums and spiritists of the land?

_____

_____

B. Why do you think Saul disguised himself before he went to the witch at Endor?

_____

_____

C. How did Samuel feel when brought up from the dead? What did he tell Saul?

_____

_____

"SAUL AND THE WITCH OF ENDOR"
BENJAMIN WEST (1738–1820)

D. What observations do you have of Benjamin West's painting of this story?

_____

_____

23. In what areas do you have a tendency to make a partial turn instead of a full U-turn? What are your "pet" sins that you minimize so you can keep them close?

_____

_____

Pray through Psalm 139:23–24 for yourself:

> Search me, O God, and know my heart;
>   test me and know my anxious thoughts.
> See if there is any offensive way in me,
>   and lead me in the way everlasting.

24. What did God impress upon your heart? What will you do about it?

_____

_____

Day 5

PICK UP YOUR MAT AND WALK

(Kathy) I struggled with bulimia for ten years, abusing laxatives and nearly destroying my health. I *had* to have help to get out of my quicksand. I went through six counselors before I

found a wonderful woman who was truly able to help me. She would often point to my gut and tell me we had to get to the real reason for my bulimia. Though I *thought* I went to her for my bulimia, when I addressed the core problems, the bulimia fell away and I was finally free.

(Dee) In many cases, we may not need counseling, but just a heart that is eager to hear and obey God. I struggled in my marriage for the first five years. I spent five years "walking in the sand," staying in a rut. But finally pain caused me to hear God, and I obeyed, being supportive of my husband instead of constantly complaining. God truly changed our relationship. In our case, God was our counselor, but I might have gotten out more quickly had I sought a Christian counselor. It takes humility to reach out for a helping hand.

Many *stay stuck* for a lifetime. In the first incident we will study today, a man had been lame for thirty-eight years when Jesus asked him some penetrating questions.

Review your memory passage.

25. Read John 5:1–15.

A. How long had the man been an invalid?_____

B. What question did Jesus ask him in verse 6? _____

_____

When the man addressed Jesus, it was as "Sir." Dr. Darrel Bock points out that the paralytic "never acknowledged Jesus as Lord but instead reported Jesus to the authorities."[3]

C. What excuses did the man give for not getting into the pool?

_____

D. What did Jesus tell the man in verse 8? What was the result?

_____

E. How might you apply this to your life?

_____

F. What warning did Jesus give the man later (v. 14)?

_____

Jesus was probably referring to the final judgment. (See John 5:28–29.) Though we are not saved through obedience, obedience is evidence of genuine faith.

G. What similar warning is given in 1 John 2:24–25?

_____

26. Do you have a sin that has kept you in bondage for a long time? If so, what is it? (You do not need to share this in the group.) If so, what excuses have you given? How would you answer the question "Do you want to get well?"

_____

_____

27. How might you apply this lesson to your life?

_____

_____

The man in the above story was "stuck" for thirty-eight years. The Israelites wandered in the desert for forty years. A whole lifetime can be wasted if we do not address the deceitfulness of our hearts and take action.

28. Read Hebrews 3:7–19.

A. What was the primary mistake these believers made according to verses 7–8?

_____

B. What basic warning is given in verse 12?

_____

C. How can we help each other according to verse 13? What would this look like in your friendships? In your small group?

_____

_____

29. We don't have to stay stuck. We have the mighty power of God in us. Read 1 John 2:12–14 and list some of the resources that John reminds believers (no matter their level of maturity) they have in Christ.

_____

_____

_____

30. What is your primary "takeaway" from this week's lesson? How will you apply it?

_____

Personal Evaluation Questions

(No one will be asked to share in the group, but this form may further your spiritual growth.)

Being set free from some strongholds in our lives may require a Christian counselor's help. But in many areas, if you immerse yourself in God's Word, come before His searching light, and are honest with your closest sisters in Christ (for prayer and accountability) you will be able to genuinely repent, to "pick up your mat" and eventually find yourself healed. Grade yourself as "excellent," "good," or "fail" on how well you are staying in the light:

A. I spend time in the Word regularly and seek God as I do: _____

B. I come before Him and ask Him, "How is it between us?" on a regular basis:_____

C. I am not trying to obey in my own strength but, instead, I am allowing His power and grace to work through me. _____

D. I am honest with my closest sisters and brothers about my struggles, making myself vulnerable and accountable to them: _____

E. I pray for my sisters who do the same with me and keep their confidences: _____

What sins defeat you again and again—keeping you stuck? Ask God for wisdom. Do you need a Christian counselor? Or do you need to simply "pick up your mat" by doing the above things and obeying? What does He show you?

_____

Prayer Time

Cluster in small groups. Look at your answer to question 31. Be willing to lift it up and allow the women to pray for you.

If you know the following praise chorus based on 1 John 4:4, you may want to close with it:

Greater is He that is in me
Greater is He that is in me
Greater is He that is in me
than he that is in the world.

Words and Music by Lanny Wolfe ©1973 Lanny Wolfe Music Co. All Rights Reserved. Used by Permission.

"I tell you the truth, unless a kernel of wheat falls to the ground and dies, it remains only a single seed. But if it dies, it produces many seeds." (JOHN 12:24)

AUTUMN GLORY

(Kathy)

It was October in Virginia, and I was visiting Ellie and her family. When I awakened one morning I found the house completely empty. Still in my pajamas, I savored the quietness as I made some coffee and sat down at the kitchen table facing a huge bay window, marveling at the breathtaking autumn scene. There were still many leaves on the trees, but just as many on the ground. Like a child, I began to count the colors outside the window: fifteen, twenty, thirty . . . Just when I thought I was done, another shade caught my eye—so many different greens, yellows, and reds. The most gifted painter couldn't possibly capture what God displayed that morning before my eyes.

All these brilliant colors made the yard look so alive. As I was admiring the picture outside the window, I was reminded that there was a process of dying going on. In the midst of the splendor, each leaf would soon fall, decay, and turn the color of death. In a month the trees would be bare, the ground barren. It would be hard to imagine the backyard vibrant with color again, but new life would emerge in the spring.

Jesus Christ gives us many invitations. He invites us to relationship with Him, to "pleasant places," and to an eternal banquet. One of the mysteries of our faith is that with all the wonderful invitations, He also invites us to die. This is the part of our Christianity that is hard for the Christian and foolish to the world. There's no way around it:

Christianity involves the Cross.

Without the Cross, there is no victory for the Christian.

When God invites us to die, it is so a resurrection can come.

VIDEO NOTES FOR WEEK 6
AUTUMN GLORY

Thoughts I want to remember:

_____

_____

_____

1. One of the mysteries of our faith is that with all the wonderful invitations, God also invites us to _____.

2. Ami Carmichael, missionary to India, talked about "a chance _____ _____."

3. God rolls stones away. With every death there is a _____.

4. *Do not love the _____ or anything in the world. If anyone loves the world, the love of the _____ is not in him.* (1 John 2:15)

5. The lust of the _____.

   The lust of the _____.

   The _____ of life.

THE LUST OF THE FLESH

The Greek word *sarx* means "bodily appetites."

> *Rejoice in the wife of your youth*
> *. . . May her breasts satisfy you always,*
> *may you ever be captivated by her love.*
> (Proverbs 5:18b–19)

6. God's gifts, such as food and sex, are enjoyed fully when we live within the

   b_____.

THE LUST OF THE EYES

The "lust of the eyes" refers to our desire to acquire things, to greed. Abraham is an example of holding both material things and people loosely.

> *He lived in tents . . . For he was looking forward to the city . . . whose architect and builder is God.* (Hebrews 11:9b–10)

7. *The world and its desires _____ _____,*
   but the man who does the will of God lives forever. (1 John 2:17)

THE PRIDE OF LIFE

8. What is the pride of life? It's wanting

   P_____ ,

   P_____ , and

   P_____ .

9. For all of us, when we look at any addiction, we need to peel off the layers and look at the _____ we are choosing that addiction.

10. Beth Moore says we need to p_____ our v_____.

ICEBREAKER *(Hear from two or three women for each question.)*

1. Think of something that you bought or did in your life that really seemed quite important to you at the time, but now, as you look back, seems like a big waste of money or time. What was it? Did you learn anything from this? If so, what?

   _____

   _____

2. What stood out to you in the video? Why?

   _____

Day 1

DO NOT LOVE THE WORLD

(Kathy) Believe me, I have a lot more dying to do, but I've seen what happens in the places where I have allowed God to take me to the cross. Chains have fallen, freedom has come, and the Spirit of the living God has breathed life into my soul and into the souls of others. I have greatly admired believers who have learned the secret of dying—individuals like Billy Graham, Mother Teresa. . . . You can almost touch Jesus in their person because of their God-centeredness, their way of speaking, their way of answering people in interviews. Many of us have had those dinner conversations where questions are asked such as, "Who would you consider to be your hero?" It doesn't have to be someone of international prominence. In fact, we love it when people say, "My mother, my sister, my friend. . . ." The people we think of are people who are so filled with love and integrity, they leave a legacy that cannot pass away. They are the believers John is describing when he says, "The world and its desires pass away, but the man who does the will of God lives forever" (1 John 2:17).

(Dee) When John tells us in 1 John 2:15, "Do not love the world," it is important to understand that he is referring neither to the created world, which God created for us to enjoy, nor to the people in the world, for God so loved the people in the world that He gave His only Son for them. Instead, as commentator John Stott explains, it is "the evil world system" and the false values they hold dear that we are to put to death.

The Message says, "Don't love the world's ways. Don't love the world's goods. Love of the world squeezes out love for the Father" (1 John 2:15).

1. Explain how "love for the world squeezes out love for the Father."

_____

_____

Jesus says, "You cannot serve both God and Money" (Luke 16:13c). When you love the values of the world, you cannot love God. When you cannot love God, you cannot love people. When you give your heart to "the lust of the flesh," you use people instead of loving them. When you give your heart to "the lust of the eyes," you are so intent on acquiring things that you neglect people or use them to get what you want. And when you give your heart to becoming powerful, you put yourself, not God and not others, first. Instead of being vibrant with the colors of His love, you are a faded believer, like the brown chaff that the wind blows away. Meditate on J. B. Phillips's paraphrase:

Never give your hearts to this world or to any of the things in it. A man cannot love the Father and love the world at the same time. For the whole world system, based as it is on men's primitive desires, their greedy ambitions and the glamour of all that they think splendid, is not derived from the Father at all, but from the world itself. The world and all its passionate desires will one day disappear. But the man who is following God's will is part of the permanent and cannot die. (1 John 2:15–17 PHILLIPS)

2. What stands out to you in J. B. Phillips's paraphrase? Why?

_____

_____

Believers who have not experienced the power of dying to themselves *want* to be happy (who doesn't?), but shades of gloom continue to color their days. They *want* to have victory over the sin that binds them, but the blackness of their sin always seems to overcome the light. They *want* to know peace, but they are overwhelmed by the turbulent circumstances of life. They *want* to have joyful intimacy in their marriage, but somehow it eludes them. Sins like pride, anger, bitterness, or a drive for wealth and status may be consuming them in such a way that they are *more* miserable than those who don't know Christ. Once you've tasted and seen that the Lord is good, He will always be whispering, wooing you to the cross, because He knows your only hope for life is in death: death to self, death to sinful passions, and death to all that the world holds so dear. Until we die, we cannot live.

Again, when the Scriptures urge us to die to ourselves, it isn't to suffer for suffering's sake, as if that's the measure of a saint. It is for more glorious things: an abundant life and a passionate heart, intimacy with God and one another, peace that passes understanding, a complete joy—all the jewels that John promised in the beginning of his letter and more. Don't trade the glory of God in your life for anything!

3. On the basis of Psalm 92:12–14, describe the believer who learns how to die to the false values of the world.

_____

_____

4. Read 1 John 2:15–17. John divides the evil world system into three parts. Give examples of each:

A. "The lust of the flesh" (KJV). The Greek word *sarx* has to do with bodily appetites. List some good desires that can become lustful desires. How might the lust of the flesh sap your strength, your ability to "flourish like a palm tree" or a green cedar?

_____

_____

Tomorrow we are going to tell you Andrea's story, a young woman who learned to die to her flesh in the area of homosexuality. We are excited to tell you her story to illustrate that God has the power to break any chains, but also because Andrea provides a model for us in overcoming the chains of the flesh, whatever they are: gluttony, addictions, sexual immorality, excessive comfort, or sloth. We are also excited because Andrea illustrates so beautifully that from death comes a beautiful new life.

B. "The lust of the eyes" (KJV). This refers to our tendency to covet and our desire for things. How might this keep you from flourishing like a palm tree and cause the efforts of your life to burn up, like hay and stubble?

_____

_____

(Dee) In this last year, Steve and I each lost a parent, and that required going through their material possessions with siblings. What freedom there is in realizing that none of the furniture, clothes, or dishes matter because all things *are* going to pass away—so if our siblings want *any* of the items, we can joyfully say, "Take it!" Remember how Jesus responded when two brothers came to Him quarreling about their inheritance? Basically He told them they just didn't get it—they didn't understand what *life* was really about (Luke 12:13–15).

C. "The pride of life" (KJV). How hard it is not to want the praise of man, to want power, popularity, and position. Repeatedly in Scripture we are told we do things either for the praise of man or the praise of God. What did Jesus say to those who did things for the praise of man and to those who did things for the praise of God (Matthew 6:1–5)?

_____

_____

Review your memory passages from the first five weeks.

Day 2

HOW DO WE DIE TO OURSELVES?

Today we will tell you Andrea's story. (You can read a more complete version in the book that is the basis of this curriculum. Also, information on how to contact Andrea or Richard can be found in the back of this book under Resources.)

Andrea's chains were chains that many think are too heavy to be broken: the chains of homosexuality. Yet today she bears the radiant colors of His love in her person, is very happily married, and is breathing life into others who are still cold and gray. Andrea is a living testimony of all that John has been promising will happen if we learn how to submit ourselves to Jesus. Andrea's story isn't just a story about breaking free from homosexuality. The principles that helped her could be applied to those in bondage to an eating disorder, a bad temper, greed, envy, laziness, a critical spirit, or any of the hundreds of addictions that go against God's will for us.

But there is another reason we want to tell you Andrea's story. The church has failed miserably when it comes to loving those in bondage to homosexuality. Jesus ate with prostitutes and thieves, and the Pharisees condemned Him. Are we going to be like the Pharisees? Jesus was compassionate, so we must be too. Sometimes we get confused, thinking that if we love the one in chains we are condoning the sin. We think that if we move close, if we listen, we are allowing that person to feel better about their bondage when, in reality, listening with a compassionate heart can prepare that person to receive the truth of Christ.

As you read Andrea's story, note what part the compassion of believers played in her release. Also, note how Andrea's deliverance was definitely a process, and Jesus was a mighty Rescuer for her, but Andrea had to surrender to Him. The same is true for you, no matter your sin.

Andrea's story begins when she was just seven. It was then that her father began to come into her bedroom, lock the door, and molest her.

> *I was living in terror and trauma twenty-four hours a day, knowing that at any moment I could be abused. I associated femaleness with weakness, because my dad was overpowering me, night after night, and my mother wasn't rescuing me.*

One of the entries for strongholds of sin is generational sin. It is particularly common in homosexuality, though not the only cause. Often, good counseling can uncover generational sin, and that insight can be the first blow to the chains that bind us. In Andrea's case, instead of getting counseling, she simply tried to live a "normal life" in her own strength. She married, but was repulsed by the marriage bed, and the marriage ended in divorce. Shortly after this, while teaching at a university, Andrea met a woman who really listened to her, sympathized with her wounds, and embraced her.

> *It felt so wonderful to have someone really care, really listen. An intensity came into our relationship that was exciting. I even thought,* Thank God she's not a man, or I'd be having an affair. *The sexual feelings began to come forth, and I constructed a rationalization. At that time, I was into Buddhism, so I told myself I was a man who had been reincarnated in a woman's body.*

Satan looped a chain around Andrea through generational sin and then tightened that chain with the deceit of Buddhism. Andrea entered into a homosexual affair.

Andrea's story here takes a wonderful turn, for the parents of the woman with whom she was having an affair loved the Lord deeply. How would you respond if one of your children had a homosexual lover? This couple, who happened to be Catholic charismatics, prayed and loved Andrea into the kingdom. Andrea remembers feeling surrounded by the love of Jesus when she was in their home.

> *They were wonderful Italians who always had room at their table for one more mouth to feed. They would invite me to church, and it was this wild, born-again church—something I had never experienced in my life and didn't understand—but there was something about it I loved. After church I'd come home with them and sit at their table and tell them about Buddhism and Taoism. They listened and simply showed me acceptance and the grace of God. It blew my mind.*
>
> *I watched their joy, their love, and their trust in adversity. This was a family who struggled to make ends meet, and the dad worked three jobs so that the mom could stay at home with the five kids. When the last kid left, they finally could afford a brand-new car—a cheap red Chevette. Right after they got it, somebody ran a red light and plowed into them. They got it fixed, and it happened again. I mocked them, saying, "Is this how God takes care of you?" But they were absolutely confident of His love and knew that somehow it would all work out for the good. And though they looked like total fools, it stuck with me.*

This couple continued to be the love of Christ to Andrea. Their prayers, their love, and their trust in God provided the slow and widening light for Andrea. She put her trust in Christ, and the affair with their daughter ended.

5. What stood out to you about the couple that reached out, with the love of Christ, to Andrea? What can you learn from them?

_____

_____

For two weeks Andrea sailed along, believing what she had heard in a sermon:

If you want to be set free, all you have to do is come to Christ.

Wouldn't that be sweet? But just as Kathy didn't wake up a size six the morning after she came to Christ, and I didn't wake up a terrific wife and mother, Andrea didn't wake up freed from her sexual addiction. The power of God was now within her, but there was still sin in her members, and the battle raged.

How do we die to ourselves and our sinful ways? It's a process, such as the one leaves go through as they change color. You don't wake up one morning and see a glorious autumn. It happens gradually. In early September you may see the tinge of red on a few leaves, then perhaps a whole tree, like a burning bush, amid the others. But one day the whole forest and the hills are ablaze with color. It's the same way with us.

Freedom takes time. Good counsel, being immersed in God's Word, vigilance, and a day-by-day setting your hand to the plow brings freedom. In some cases, you will realize you are truly free. The chains are gone. In others, you may not be truly free until heaven, but the shackles are loosened, and there is hope instead of despair.

Though God wanted Andrea to be set free, she didn't know how to stop the cycle. She would sin, repent, and sin again. It was the struggle we all have experienced with some kind of sin, the struggle Paul described when he said:

When I want to do good, evil is right there with me. For in my inner being I delight in God's law; but I see another law at work in the members of my body, waging war against the law of my mind and making me a prisoner of the law of sin at work within my members. What a wretched man I am! Who will rescue me from this body of death? (Romans 7:21–24)

6. What was the battle that Paul experienced? Have you experienced this? Where? (You don't need to share with the group.)

_____

_____

Andrea had to learn, as we all do, what was her part, and what was God's part. God is on our side. We must keep wrestling with Him, the way Jacob did. Andrea kept crying out to Him.

I was reading testimonies from those who had been set free. I remember in one book the author said that when we sin, whatever it is, we are being cannibals. We are eating others alive, destroying their hearts. That image stayed with me. I read that book when I was having my third affair. In my first two affairs, the women meant something to me. Now it was just a "summer fling." I was just using this woman because of my addiction. I was becoming my father. I was a cannibal: destroying another person in order to feed my flesh.

The "cannibal" image portrays *the heart* of what John's letter teaches. If we do not walk in the light, if we do not die to ourselves, *we end up destroying our brothers.* Instead of becoming like God, who gives life, we become like our enemy, who was a murderer from the beginning.

God didn't give up on Andrea. Just as Hosea kept going after Gomer, the Lord kept going after Andrea. His Spirit continued to wrestle with her, through Scripture, through godly friends, and through His still, small voice, speaking the truth to her. Andrea said:

> *One night the Lord spoke to me. He said, "What would your obituary say? How diminished your life is. What gods are you serving?"*

That was the moment Andrea stopped choosing to sin. God had spoken to her many times and in many ways, but that was the turning point. After that pivotal moment, she never returned to her sin. That's not to say her life was without temptation, but that she kept moving higher and higher up the ladder, closer and closer to the light.

> *I began to dialogue with God, asking Him what was His part? What was my part? It was a very sweet time, and just as God hedged Gomer in for a time, so that she couldn't sin, there was a period of nine months when God simply protected me from temptation while I began to get stronger. It was amazing grace.*
>
> *I knew I had to keep His truth pouring into my soul. I read* The Living Bible *in the format of* The Life Application Bible *and just kept dialoguing with God, asking Him to show me, to help me.*

One analogy that has been helpful to us is that God's truth is like the sap that rises in the spring, bringing new life to the trees. There are always those *stubborn* leaves that have refused to die, that have tenaciously clung to the branches all winter, but when the sap rises in the spring, it pushes them off. The truth of God's Word can have the same effect.

Whatever our struggle is, the same questions need to be asked: What is my part? What is God's part? What light can God's Word shed on this? The same questions apply, whatever your struggle happens to be.

PERSONAL EXERCISE
(Will not be shared in the group)

7. Dialogue with God about the struggle you mentioned in question 6. What is your part? What is God's part? Be still before Him and write down anything He impresses on your heart. Plan your victory for today. What will be your strategy?

_____

_____

Andrea continues:

> *A passage that became very meaningful to me was Romans 12:1–2. I began to realize I could really have the mind of Christ, that He could be incarnated through me, and that was so exciting. It also said,*
>
> *"Then you will learn from your own experience how his ways will really satisfy you"* (Romans 12:2b TLB).

This truth that Andrea discovered is terribly significant. The reason we are unwilling to die to something is because we don't believe God's ways can truly satisfy us. Do you see that in the above verse? John Piper, in *Desiring God*, pleads:

> *Take all your self-love—all your longing for joy and hope and love and security and fulfillment and significance—take all that and focus it on God, until he satisfies your heart and soul and mind. This is not a canceling out of self-love. This is a fulfillment of self-love. . . . God says, "Come to me and I will give you fullness of joy" (Psalm 16:11). . . . And with that great discovery—that God is the never-ending fountain of our joy, the way we love others is forever changed.*[1]

So often our area of ministry becomes the area where we have been set free. Andrea began counseling those still in the chains of homosexuality. One weekend Andrea went to a leaders' conference on sexual addictions. Rich was there, representing a ministry in Philadelphia. When Andrea walked in, Rich noticed her immediately. He said:

> *She was striking. Her countenance was one of confidence. Unfortunately, a lot of the people who are in leadership in this field still have a lot of woundedness. She was different. I wondered, Who is she?*

Unbeknownst to Andrea, Rich had prayed that if he were ever to marry, it would have to be someone who had been delivered from homosexuality, for she would truly be able to understand *where* he had been and *how* he had been set free. Though John 8:36 promises that "if the Son sets you free, you will be free indeed," many doubt that it can really happen in the area of homosexuality. So Rich longed for someone who *knew*, from her own experience, the *reality* of that freedom.

And unbeknownst to Rich, Andrea had told friends that if she were ever to marry, she wanted it to be someone standing clear on the other side of homosexuality, who was truly free. She longed for a husband who was willing to be a missionary, helping those still in bondage. Andrea watched Rich in amazement, seeing his heart for the lost, seeing his desire to be a father to the fatherless, seeing his great joy in the Lord. Rich watched Andrea, seeing her compassion, her wisdom, and her ability to articulate so clearly and so sensitively the truths of God. Rich and Andrea soon found themselves spending a lot of time together. Andrea said:

> *Our courtship was a beautiful drawing together—there were not lights and whistles at first, but a relationship founded in Christ. It really wasn't about us. It was about God. He was*

drawing us together. We each were truly content in our singleness, yet it was so clear that God was drawing us together.

One night I was at a conference called Living Water, and a woman prayed a prophetic prayer over me, saying, "God is awakening you."

Shortly after that Rich and I definitely began coming out of our deep sleep.

Andrea said that on her wedding day she flew into the heavenlies, and she hasn't landed. Andrea and Rich are a picture of innocence restored, of captives set free. Andrea glowed as she said:

When I was a little girl, probably just four, somebody told me enough about Jesus that I would pretend He was with me, playing with me in a grove of pine trees, running about and laughing with me. Now, in a beautiful way, I feel like I have my playmate again, and I am free and innocent, like a child.

Beautiful things happen on the other side of dying. There is an unspeakable joy and a sweet contentment in being right with God.

8. What do you think you will remember from Andrea's story? _____

_____

Begin learning your memory passage.

Day 3

OVERCOMING THE LUST OF THE FLESH

(Kathy) I am inspired by the stories of Joseph and Moses, and how both refused "to enjoy the pleasures of sin for a short time" (Hebrews 11:25). Refusing to enjoy the "pleasures of sin"—a choice. What a war the flesh wages against the spirit! As long as I breathe I will deal with my passions and have to continually die to the ones that are not directed toward God. For example, during the height of my struggle with bulimia, there were many days when I craved sweets and salt and would go from Oreos to French fries and back to Oreos. . . . It would definitely have an effect on my body and my emotions the next day: I'd get bogged down; my ambition went out the window; I became a slug. There was a continual challenge every day for me to "choose the next right thing," to look at the reasons why I was "stuffing my body." Even though there was momentary pleasure, it robbed me of joy, of a healthy self-esteem in God, and of living in a sober state of being at peace with the Lord. We must constantly die to the momentary pleasures that throw us into darkness.

Joseph provides a helpful model in overcoming the lust of the flesh. Read this incident carefully, looking for both his mind set and his action. Joseph had been sold into slavery by his jealous brothers, but he had gained the trust of Potiphar, a chief officer of the pharaoh.

9. Read Genesis 39:2–12.

A. What did Potiphar, the Egyptian master, observe in the life of Joseph (v. 2–3)?

_____

_____

Joseph exemplifies John's principle that if we walk in the light, we will have genuine intimacy with God. When we leave the light, we leave God's fellowship, for God cannot come with us into the darkness.

B. List some of the ways God had blessed Joseph (vv. 3–6).

_____

_____

C. Describe the temptation (vv. 7, 10).

_____

_____

D. Describe Joseph's mind set. What was his primary reason for refusing her? What does this tell you about Joseph?

_____

_____

E. Describe Joseph's actions (vv. 10b–12).

_____

_____

Charles Spurgeon, the great English preacher, spoke of this incident:

Like a true hero, as he was, [he] said to her, "How can I do this great wickedness and sin against God?" Like a wise warrior, he knew that in such a case fleeing was the better part of valour. He heard a voice in his ears, "Fly, Joseph, fly; there remains no way of victory but flight."

To be haunted day by day by solicitations of the softest kind—to be tempted hour by hour— Oh! it needs a strength superangelic, a might more than human, a strength which only God can grant, for a young man thus to cleanse his way, and take heed thereto according to God's word. Oh! there was a power indeed within that heart of his; there was an inconceivable might, which made him turn away with unutterable disgust, with fear and trembling, while he said, "How can I? How can I—God's Joseph—how can I—other men might, but how can I do this great wickedness and sin against God?" [2]

F. What temptations of the flesh whisper to you, day after day? What could you learn from Joseph that would strengthen you to do what is right? Be very specific.

_____

_____

_____

"JOSEPH AND POTIPHAR'S WIFE"
ORAZIO GENTILESCHI (1563–1639)

10. What thoughts do you have as you meditate on the above painting?

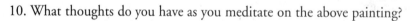
_____

_____

(Kathy) There are always sexual temptations for a single woman, as I'm sure there are for married women too. I must continually die to immediate gratification. It helps greatly for me to be accountable to those closest to me. But the core reason that helps me to flee temptations of the flesh is expressed in Joseph's words: *How could I do this great sin against God?* This makes me think about my responsibility to live faithfully for Christ and to be an ambassador of the gospel. If I fall, how many women would be hurt who are looking to me? So when tempted I must ask, *"Why* would I do this great sin?" We must be aware of the consequences of our choices and cling to the Lord as our protection, our fortress against the enemy.

In her song "Generations," Sara Groves writes how she can pass on a curse or a blessing to future generations, knowing her choices will affect her great-great-great-granddaughter. Joseph's choice, though it caused him pain, eventually brought him, and generations to come, great blessings. Temptations of the flesh are *so* immediate, but the consequences go on and on.

When you are being tempted, whether by a scene on a video, a married man at work, or a substance (alcohol, chocolate, marijuana . . .) that you have abused in the past, you are walking right toward a steep precipice. The precipice is much steeper than the enemy would have you believe. The fall will be costly. *Remember*, Satan is a deceiver.

In the heat of the moment, it is often hard to think clearly. So now, when you are cool, think about the consequences. Then ask the Spirit to bring these to your remembrance the next time you are tempted.

11. List some of the consequences for you if you were to give in to the areas in which you are tempted by the lust of the flesh. Give both short-term and long-term consequences. (Consider how you are passing on sin in the form of behaviors or attitudes to future generations.)

_____

_____

_____

12. List some of the blessings, some of the "beautiful colors" that will come to your life if you live within God's boundaries concerning bodily appetites. Give both short-term and long-term blessings. (Consider how you are passing on grace to future generations.)

_____

_____

_____

13. What teachings impress you from Proverbs 5:15–23?

_____

_____

14. Why does 1 Corinthians 6:18–20 tell us to flee in the area of sexual temptation?

_____

_____

15. Meditate on James 4:4–9.

A. What warning can be found in verse 4? What similarity do you see to 1 John 2:15?

_____

_____

B. Find three promises and three conditions for the promises in verses 6, 7, and 8.

_____

_____

_____

16. What have you learned that can help you overcome the lust of the flesh?

_____

_____

Review your memory passage.

Day 4

OVERCOMING THE LUST OF THE EYES

(Dee) The lust of the eyes refers to our acquisitive desires, thinking the things we see can fill up the emptiness in our hearts. Generally this has to do with material possessions: houses, land, clothes, and all kinds of toys. As a young woman, I struggled greatly with the lust of the eyes, for I was consumed with the desire to have a *Better Homes and Gardens* house overlooking the Pacific Ocean. Yet when I died to that, when I laid down that desire, amazing blessings followed. It freed my thoughts and turned them to eternal matters. It freed my husband to join a Christian medical practice in rural Nebraska. The states lining the Pacific Coast are beautiful, but the need for doctors is slim. In rural Nebraska, Steve is truly needed. Each night he feels so satisfied in being used of God to bring relief and healing to the good-hearted farmers suffering from back pain.

Blessings that I never anticipated flowed from my simple "death." Not only have we grown to love Nebraska, but also we have been so strengthened by the godly people with whom Steve practices. The other night at supper the five doctors and their wives were listing the spiritual blessings we have seen over the years and we were all close to tears. My husband is the kind of man that would have given me that ocean house had I persisted, but oh, what a tremendous price we would have paid. I believe that my covetousness would have quenched the spiritual flame I saw beginning in my husband. I remember how proud I felt of him when, as a brand-new Christian, he enthusiastically led a Sunday school class full of men in a simple children's chorus:

> *Happiness is to know the Savior*
> *Living a life within His favor*
> *Having a change in my behavior*
> *Happiness is the Lord*

Words and Music by Ira F. Stanphil © 1968 Singspiration Music/ ASCAP.

What if I had quenched that flame with the deceitfulness of riches? Instead, I have seen that flame grow into a fire, impacting generations to come. Recently our four-year-old grandson, Simeon, was disappointed in a dump truck Steve had given him, for Simeon had really wanted a tractor. Simeon said,

"Grampa, did you remember I wanted a tractor?"

Steve said, "Simeon, I tried to find one at Wal-Mart, but I couldn't."

Simeon pouted. "Did you look really, really hard?"

Steve hesitated, feeling that he had disappointed Simeon, and then thought, *No. This is a teachable moment.* Gently, Steve said,

"Simeon, only Jesus can make you happy."

After Kathy and I had taped this session on the video, I made a lighthearted comment off-camera about how much nicer Kathy's suit was than mine. Appropriately, one of the women in the audience checked me, saying with a smile:

"Dee, only Jesus can make you happy."

17. What are some of the material things you imagine might make you happy? Review what John says about the desires of this world in 1 John 2:15–17 and write down how you might talk to yourself!

_____

_____

_____

If you know the following praise chorus, sing it to the Lord in your time alone with Him.

Seek ye first the Kingdom of God
and His righteousness,
and all these things will be added unto you.
Allelu, Alleluia.

18. Abraham is a wonderful example of overcoming the lust of the eyes. Read Hebrews 11:8–19.

A. Describe Abraham's housing and why he was content with it (vv. 8–10).

_____

B. Is there an application to your life?

_____

C. What did Abraham believe about God and how was he blessed (vv. 11–12)?

_____

D. How did Abraham and the believers like him view their lives (v. 13)?

_____

E. Is there an application to your life?

_____

F. What promise is given in verse 16 to those who die to the lust of the eyes?

_____

G. How did Abraham demonstrate that he loved God even more than his only son (vv. 17–18)?

_____

"THE ANGEL STOPPING ABRAHAM
FROM SACRIFICING ISAAC"
REMBRANDT (1606–1669)

H. What thoughts do you have as you contemplate Rembrandt's masterpiece?

_____

I. Why was Abraham able to obey God and offer Isaac as a sacrifice (v. 19)?

_____

_____

Abraham waited so long for his son Isaac. Sara was old and had been barren for years. If anyone had a reason to cling too tightly to a child and to worship him, Abraham did. But though Abraham deeply loved his wife and his son, his source of fulfillment was God. He delighted in God, he trusted that God would do what was best for his loved ones, and so he obeyed God. When the Lord told him to sacrifice Isaac, he headed out to obey. Oh, to have that immediate and passionate response to the Almighty!

(Dee) As a parent, I simply cannot imagine doing what Abraham did. But sometimes God puts us in a situation where we simply don't have a choice. Twice in my life I have had to abandon a child to God, because they were simply in a situation I could not fix. Once it was with a son who was a prodigal, and all I could do was fast and pray. Another time involved our daughter Sally, who was in a spiritually abusive relationship for many years.

Do you know what I found out? God is a better parent than I could ever be. When I stopped trying to fix it and abandoned my children to Him, He was a Mighty Warrior on their behalf, rescuing each of them. I belong to a faithful God who can raise the dead! I am His Beloved, and His banner over me, and over my children, is love.

19. What or whom is God asking you to relinquish to Him? Do you trust Him enough to do it?

_____

_____

20. Read Genesis 22:1–18 and write down verses that tell you something about Abraham's attitude toward God. How did this help him not to cling to the things of this world?

_____

_____

21. What have you learned that will help you to hold the things and the people of this world loosely?

_____

_____

Review your memory passage.

OPEN WIDE YOUR MOUTH AND I WILL FILL IT

Next week we will consider the third lust, "the pride of life." But because it is so easy to get consumed with the "thou shalt nots," we want to remind you of the "thou shalls!" Most important of all is to love Jesus. John Piper tells us to take our self-love, to take our lusts, and to *focus* on God until He satisfies our heart and soul and mind.

So often we'll go through our days lifting a cup in the air, saying, "Fill me, fill me." We have so many soul needs. But only Jesus can truly satisfy us. Instead of using things, people, or your position in life to get the love you want, find it in God and in His pleasure in you.

(Dee) I have seen enormous spiritual growth in my precious daughter-in-law, Julie Brestin. When she was in her early twenties, she reminded me so much of myself at that age, often thinking the things "under the sun" could fulfill her. Yet I saw her come to a crossroads more than once, when she was tempted to take a job outside the home because of a wonderful offer. Each time, she "died." She couldn't work outside the home *and* be at home with her four young children, so she turned down a prestigious offer and a second income. But she didn't just say *no* to the world, she said *yes* to God, immersing herself in His Word, in teaching her children, and equipping other young women in ministry.

Now Julie is in her early thirties, and I am seeing the beauty of those choices, like the splendor of autumn. Her children are little disciples, and Julie has the things John's letter promises: intimacy with God, intimacy with believers, and a fullness of joy. In the same way, Julie has also shed thirty pounds, going from a size 12 to a size 6. What is her secret? Again, she has focused on the Lord. Yes, she had to discipline herself, and there were plenty of "deaths" to gratifying her flesh. She knows her heart can deceive her into how much she is actually eating, so she counted Weight Watcher points. But her primary *focus* has been on Jesus, panting for Him as a deer pants for water. She has been willing to *wait* for Him to satisfy her longings, and He has met her and satisfied her heart and soul and mind.

Though Julie is a busy homeschooling mom of four, she says she cannot wait to get up in the morning and fly into the arms of Jesus. She gave me permission to share a little of one of her recent letters:

> God is so amazing to me I just want to explode. I cannot believe His brilliance. My husband laughs at my excitement. I literally jump out of bed when the alarm goes off at 5:00 because I can't wait to be in the presence of God. Please pray for my protection as I know that the devil is on to me. Pray that I will not take even the tiniest measure of glory for myself, which is a putrid thought to me. I have such a desire for women to have a passion for the Word like I do, and it is contagious. I literally have women lined up who want me to mentor them and teach them how to study God's Word. I have neighbors coming over wanting to know why I'm so different. We also have an exchange student from the Ukraine living with

us who recently accepted the Lord and has studied the Bible with me. I hear her singing praise songs in her bedroom.

This morning a lady from church who is sad from her circumstances came to pray with me. After we spent time at the foot of God's throne, with tears running down her face, in astonishment she said, "I felt Him!"

I said, "You just got a hug from God." And we praised Him. I AM TRULY AMAZED! My jumping out of bed stems not only from my excitement, but also from my desperate need for His instructions that day! I am lost without Him!

What I am seeing in Julie is the "complete joy" that John promises as we set our affections on Him. Julie's ministry is also satisfying because it is "part of the permanent."

> *The world and all its passionate desires will one day disappear. But the man who is following God's will is part of the permanent and cannot die.* (1 John 2:17 PHILLIPS)

22. John has told us not to love the world, but it is also important, according to the above verse, to be proactive, to do something positive. What is it? How do you see this in Julie's story?

_____

_____

_____

The following story that Jesus tells in three short verses is sobering, but it is also powerful in helping us realize the importance of being proactive in loving the Lord.

23. Read Luke 11:24–26.

A. What does the evil spirit do in this story?

_____

_____

B. What is the warning?

_____

_____

> *"Demons like barren locales (Isa. 13:21; 34:14). . . . If that person does not fill the space (himself) with God, then the house is empty and vulnerable to reoccupation. Jesus' point in 11:24–26 is that if God's grace is not embraced, then the spirit will return to render even worse damage."* [3]
>
> (Dr. Darrell Bock)

We were created to worship God. If we're not worshiping Him, we will worship something else. If the true "affections of our heart" are not toward God, they will be toward something else. Therefore, though sweeping our "house clean" is good, we must immediately fill that house with the Lord by spending time with Him: reading His Word, listening to music that quickens our love for the Lord in mind and in spirit, spending time with sisters in Christ who are so overflowing with His love and His thoughts that they help us find strength in Him, and seeking ways to use our gifts to serve Him in meaningful ways. He says,

Open wide your mouth and I will fill it. (Psalm 81:10b)

Not only must we focus on the Lord, we must replace the negative behavior with a positive behavior. Often in Scripture we are told to take off the old clothes and to put on the new. If we are going to be clothed in the colors of His love, we must be intentional about it.

24. In the following passages in Ephesians 4, name the clothes that must be put off and the clothes that must be put on:

    A. Ephesians 4:25_____

    B. Ephesians 4:28_____

    C. Ephesians 4:29_____

    D. Ephesians 4:31–32_____

25. Imagine that you were counseling a younger woman who has "swept her house clean" of one of the following lusts or evil spirits. What strategy might you suggest to her so that she can "fill her house" with the Lord? (We've gotten you started.)

    A. She has swept her house clean of the soap opera she used to watch every day for an hour while her baby was napping.

    She should have a strategy, planning to make this hour a very special, intimate, and restorative one with the Lord. Next to a special chair where she will curl up will be tea, a fragrant candle, a hymnal, a Bible, and even an edifying novel. There she will sing to the Lord, with her whole heart and soul and mind. She will meditate on a psalm and pray through it. She may relax and read, guilt-free.

    B. She has swept her house clean of the covetousness that filled her heart to have what a second income could provide: nicer clothes, a bigger house, a vacation to Florida.

    _____

    _____

C. She has swept her house clean of the close friend who used to pull her down with gossip and apathy toward the things of God.

_____

_____

D. She has swept her cupboards and refrigerator clean of the chocolates and chips that tempted her to binge.

_____

_____

E. She has swept her heart clean of a complaining spirit.

_____

_____

26. What have you learned this week that stood out to you? How will you apply it to your life?

_____

_____

PRAYER TIME

Cluster in small groups. Look at your answer to the last question. Be willing to lift it up and allow the women to pray for you.

If you know the following praise chorus, close your prayer time with it:

Seek ye first the Kingdom of God
and His righteousness,
and all these things will be added unto you.
Allelu, Alleluia.

IT'S NOT EASY BEING GREEN

(Kathy)

I love living in Nashville part of the year. I've often said I think Tennessee is one of the most beautiful states. It is so green—from its lush valleys to its densely forested mountains. In the spring the branches are bursting with new buds and thick green leaves, and in the fall the colors are absolutely magnificent. During these seasons I often take drives and marvel at God's creation.

Dee and I recently discovered something interesting about the color in leaves. The powerful green of the chlorophyll dominates the whole leaf. It thrives in warm weather and hides all the other glorious colors in the leaf. But in the autumn, when the weather turns cool, the chlorophyll *dies,* and all the colors that have been hidden can be seen.

In the same way, God has created beautiful characteristics in each of us that He desires to see flourish. Those qualities can easily be hidden, like the colors in a leaf, if the overbearing "green" of pride or the fear of man dominates our person. So when we say, "It's not easy being green," we are referring to the consequences of being ruled by pride or the fear of man.

Though green *is* one of God's most beautiful and lush colors, in this chapter we'd like you to associate it with the negative characteristics of pride and the fear of man. Yet when we allow that "green" to die, the glorious colors of God's love can be seen.

VIDEO NOTES FOR WEEK 7
IT'S NOT EASY BEING GREEN

Thoughts I want to remember:

_____

_____

_____

_____

_____

1. The powerful green of the chlorophyll dominates the whole leaf. But in the autumn, when the weather turns cool, the chlorophyll d_____ , and all the beautiful colors that have been h_____ can be seen.

2. In this chapter we'd like you to associate "green" with the negative characteristics of:

_____

and

the _____ of _____.

3. *I hate _____ and arrogance.* (Proverbs 8:13b)

4. *God opposes the _____ but gives grace to the humble.* (James 4:6b)

5. In Isaiah 8:12, when God says *Do not fear what they fear,* He's talking about the fear of

_____.

6. In the book of Esther we find an ancient world obsessed with the lust of the flesh, the lust of the eyes, and the pride of life. In an almost blasphemous phrase we are told:

For a full 180 days he displayed the vast wealth of his kingdom and the

_____ *and* _____ *of his majesty.* (Esther 1:4)

7. An immoral plan is devised to replace Vashti.

Let a _____ be made for beautiful young virgins for the king.
(Esther 2:2)

In the evening she would go there and in the _____return to another part of the harem. (Esther 2:14a)

8. The word *pleases* is the same word that Samson used about the Philistine woman when he said: *"Get her for me; for she _____ me _____"* (Judges 14:3 KJV).

9. Three generations before Esther, the believers from the Holy Land were taken captive into Persia. The faith of that generation was strong. D_____ refused to stop praying and was thrown into the lion's den.

10. P_____ is like the chlorophyll in the leaves.

The f_____ of m_____ is like the chlorophyll in the leaves.

ICEBREAKER *(Hear from a few for each question.)*

1. What impressed you about the movie *The Wizard of Oz* as a child?

_____

2. In the video, Dee shares a story of how pride nearly divided her prayer group. What do you remember about this story and why?

_____

3. What else stood out to you in the video?

_____

Day 1

IT'S NOT EASY BEING QUEEN

The story of Esther begins with a six-month party. It's hard to imagine, isn't it?

The guest list was made up of the military leaders of Persia. The party of Xerxes (the Greek name for Ahasuerus) was designed to impress them. Xerxes was puffed up with his own power and importance, and the book is written subtly and satirically, quietly ridiculing the pompous attitude of both Xerxes and Haman. If you don't recognize the satire in Esther, you may miss the point. Years ago there was a television program called *All in the Family*. It ridiculed the bigotry of the father, Archie Bunker. But there were some who could not see that it was a satire, and actually admired Archie for his bigotry. In the same way, if you miss the fact that God is making fun of Xerxes, Memucan, Haman, and even Mordecai, you are going to miss much of the point of Esther. Esther beautifully illustrates the danger of "the pride of life."

It *is* a funny book, but remember, many sober truths are told in jest.

Though God makes fun of the pride of these leaders, He is not taking it lightly. Pride leads to atrocities. History reports that Xerxes often shed innocent blood, whether it was to add to his domain, to do away with a wife who displeased him, or to demonstrate that *nobody* defied the king. Polygamy sprang from "the pride of life," for it increased power and position. One incident that the historian Herodotus reports shows the depravity of Xerxes. He said that Pythius of Lydia, an extremely wealthy man, offered to finance the war Xerxes wanted to lead against Greece. The elderly statesman had one small favor to ask of Xerxes, that the eldest of his five sons be allowed to stay at home. When the men left for war, Xerxes had the eldest son of Pythius cut in half. The army marched to war between the halves of the young man's corpse. He said to Pythius, "There, now you can keep your son at home."[1] Xerxes certainly reflected the heart of his father, Satan.

Xerxes' party was more ostentatious than the most elaborate parties Hollywood has ever thrown. Even the weddings of the biggest stars would pale in comparison. It is also a party that exalts exactly what John tells us not to love:

> *The craze for sex,*
> *the ambition to buy everything that appeals to you,*

and the pride that comes from wealth and importance.
(1 John 2:16 TLB)

The purpose of the party is clearly stated in an almost blasphemous phrase:

For a full 180 days he displayed the vast wealth of his kingdom and the splendor and glory of his majesty. (Esther 1:4)

Xerxes displayed his wealth and power for six months. When the six months were over, he ended it with a seven-day banquet in his enclosed garden. Nothing was held back: Wine was served in elaborate golden goblets, the men reclined on couches of silver and gold, and the floor was a mosaic pavement of marble, mother-of-pearl, and other costly stones. (Archaeological excavations have substantiated this.) As with all things "under the sun," at first they are exciting, but soon they become boring. The only way to keep interest alive is to escalate, and Xerxes wanted to end his party with a bang. So he called for his seven eunuchs to bring in his wife, Vashti. Eunuchs were men who had been castrated to guard the queen.

One way you can measure the decadence of a country is by the way it treats its people. How sad to castrate young men, robbing them of their manhood and their hopes for a family.

And why were seven men needed to bring in *one* woman? Perhaps Xerxes anticipated resistance. What woman would *want* to appear before a drunken stag party? Perhaps it was pomp and circumstance, for they may have planned to bring Vashti in on some kind of platform. Some commentators say she was to wear only her crown (Esther 1:11). Josephus, one ancient historian, said she was to appear in the nude.[2] Whether or not this is correct, it is clear it was a demeaning request, like asking her to pop out of a cardboard cake.

(Dee) It astounds me when I hear Bible teachers say that Vashti was wrong to refuse. I think, *If this speaker knew what was really being asked of Vashti, he (or she) would never say that. Would they tell women to submit to an orgy?* Although Scripture *does* tell us to submit to our husbands, there is one exception: If your husband asks you to do something that is blatantly against God's moral law, you must refuse. You should be gracious, but you should never submit to sin.

Whatever her motivation—and we do not know her heart, for it may have been virtuous or vindictive—Vashti refuses the order. The lights don't go on. The curtains don't go up. Instead of ending his party with a bang, Xerxes is humiliated. His counselor, Memucan, is angry. You can almost see Memucan, his face flushed with rage and wine, as he sputters:

According to law, what must be done to Queen Vashti? . . . She has not obeyed the command of King Xerxes that the eunuchs have taken to her. (Esther 1:15)

The decision is made to banish Vashti. Some historians say she was deposed and others say she was beheaded. Her defiance, whatever motivated it, is very significant. Vashti took a stand—and she paid the cost.

It's not easy being queen.

1. Read Esther 1:1 through 2:18 carefully. Then answer these questions.

   A. How many provinces did Xerxes reign over (v. 1)?

   _____

This was an area bigger than the United States, stretching between the countries we identify today as India and Ethiopia. Some historians report that Xerxes *thought* he was king of the whole world, with the exception of Greece, which was the only other land mass he could see. His father had tried to conquer Greece and had failed. Xerxes was eager to succeed where his father had failed, but history tells us he lost this war devastatingly, and Persia never recovered its glory. In the power struggles in Esther, God prevails, continually exalting the humble and bringing down the proud.

   B. Describe the length and the purpose of his party (v. 4). What satire do you see in this verse? (Psalm 2 says the Lord "laughs" at kings who think they are more powerful than God.)

   _____

   C. After the six-month party, Xerxes had a seven-day drinking party for the men. Describe the wealth, the wine, and the order given to each guest (v. 5–8).

   _____

   _____

   D. Explain how Xerxes was humiliated on the seventh day of this party (v. 9–12). Put yourself in his shoes and try to imagine what he was feeling.

   _____

   _____

Read the following rendition of Memucan's words:

"It's not only the king Queen Vashti has insulted, it's all of us, leaders and people alike in every last one of King Xerxes' provinces. The word's going to get out: 'Did you hear the latest about Queen Vashti? King Xerxes ordered her to be brought before him and she wouldn't do it!' When the women hear it, they'll start treating their husbands with contempt. The day the wives of the Persian and Mede officials get wind of the queen's insolence, they'll be out of control. Is that what we want, a country of angry women who don't know their place?" (Esther 1:16–18 MSG)

   E. What was Memucan's concern? How did Xerxes respond to his advice (v. 16–22)? What humor do you see in Memucan's words?

   _____

   _____

He sent bulletins to every part of the kingdom, to each province in its own script, to each people in their own language: "Every man is master of his own house; whatever he says, goes." (Esther 1:22 MSG)

F. How would you respond if the above edict were posted outside your home? What *does* make a woman want to honor her husband?

_____

_____

G. The book of Esther is filled with satire. What humor do you see in the opening chapter?

_____

_____

H. When Xerxes is missing Vashti, what advice do the counselors give him, and how does he respond (Esther 2:1–4)?

_____

_____

I. What are the credentials for choosing the new queen (vv. 2–4)? What does this tell you about the values of ancient Persia?

_____

_____

J. What do you learn about Esther and Mordecai in 2:7?

_____

_____

K. What happened when the king's order and edict had been proclaimed (2:8)?

_____

The video that we suggest your group watch some evening (See Appendix C for information on *Esther*, produced by Trimark Video) portrays terror on the part of the virgins and grief on the part of their parents. We believe this is an accurate portrayal. There was nothing light-hearted about this contest, for it was a terrible abuse of women. We do not know how many virgins "were taken." Historian Josephus estimates 400,[3] and Paton estimates 1,460 (a virgin a night for four years).[4] We know, according to the text itself (Esther 1:1 and 2:2–3), that there were commissioners appointed in each of the 127 provinces to "search" for them.

Why did Esther *not* reveal her nationality or her family background (2:10)? On the basis of Esther 2:12, 16; and 3:13, estimate how long Esther hid her faith.

_____

In order to hide her faith, Esther probably had to eat unclean food and participate in idol worship for this length of time.

L. What does Mordecai do while Esther is in the palace (2:11)? How do you interpret his actions?

_____

M. Describe the preparations for the night with King Xerxes (2:12).

_____

In a commentary on Esther, Dr. Joyce Baldwin writes:

> *The twelve months of beauty treatment provided "marriage preparation," but the sad part was that for the majority what awaited them was more like widowhood than marriage. Though each girl in turn moved from the house of Hegai to that of Shaashgaz, once she had become a concubine, there was no guarantee that the king would remember her by name and call for her even once more.*[5]

N. Where would each virgin go when it was her turn? After that, where would she live? Would she see the king again (2:14)?

_____

_____

2. Knowing what you do about the character of Xerxes, why might it be a frightening prospect to take a stand and to refuse to participate in this contest? If you were a mother and had a daughter "taken," what feelings might you have had?

_____

_____

Begin learning your memory passage.

THE CONTROVERSY IN THE BOOK OF ESTHER

(Dee) Esther is one of the most difficult and controversial books in the Bible. I wrote an in-depth guide of the whole book called *A Woman's Journey Through Esther*. I have received so much encouraging mail about this guide, but a few letters have been angry. One woman wrote:

> *Esther has always been my heroine. How could you say the things you did about her? We won't be purchasing your guides anymore.*

Many have not looked deeply into the story of Esther, but we must. It may be appropriate for "VeggieTales" to skip the decadent sexual immorality in Esther, but adults need to see it. We cannot make accurate applications unless we see what was really happening. I believe many have missed what is actually happening in Esther because we have a tendency to think we already know what is in a passage that we have been told, especially if a story was a popular children's Bible story. Instead of reading the verses carefully on our own, we gloss over them, assuming we already know them.

Also, for many, especially the Jews, Esther and Mordecai have become objects of adulation. When the book of Esther is read among the Jews at their holiday of Purim, the children boo whenever Haman's name is read and cheer loudly whenever Esther's and Mordecai's names are read. Considering the enormous suffering of the Jewish people, it is understandable that Esther, who risked her life for her people, would be a heroine. And she is! She came to exemplify exactly what John says real love is, when he says that just as Jesus laid down His life, so are we to lay down our lives for our brothers (1 John 3:16). She came to be the shining "star" that the name Esther means.

FRESCO OF ESTHER
ANDREA DEL CASTAGNO (1423–1457)

However, it is also vital to see the *whole* story as it really happened, and to see that Esther and Mordecai may not have been such wonderful role models in the beginning. I have also received many letters from those who have thanked me for encouraging them to dig deeper, and to see things they had not seen before. One woman wrote:

> *Instead of discouraging me, seeing how Esther failed to withstand the pressures of her world in her youth has actually encouraged me. Seeing how God is a God of second chances, and how He redeemed that whole situation has given me enormous hope. Though I was a believer I had premarital sex and then an abortion. Thousands of times I have wished I could undo my sin. But I cannot. This story has given me hope that though my sin grieved the heart of God, He still can turn ashes into beauty, if I trust Him and obey Him the way Esther learned to do.*

Why is the book of Esther so controversial? It is because of the silence of God. His name is not even mentioned (the only book to have that distinction), and He makes no comments about the choices of the believers. It *isn't* unusual for a hero to fail, for Noah, Moses, Peter, and others failed. What *is* unusual is for God to be silent about the failure.

3. In the following passages, list the failure of one of God's great saints, and then show how God communicated His displeasure with His child.

   A. Genesis 12:10–20 _____

   _____

   B. 2 Samuel 11 (especially v. 27) _____

   _____

F. B. Huey Jr., in *The Expositor's Commentary,* explains that "the hiddenness of God can sometimes be explained as evidence of His displeasure" (Amos 8:11; Ezekiel 11:23).[6] God's silence means the *reader* is left to decide if Vashti was right to disobey her husband, if Esther was right to participate in the beauty contest, if Mordecai was right to refuse to show honor to the king's official, and the list goes on. Clearly, in this book, the proud are brought low and the humble are exalted. Xerxes, Haman, and Mordecai all seem to have been motivated by pride. The difference is that Mordecai humbles himself. He clearly repented, exemplifying walking in the light and *living* in repentance.

4. How does the "silence" on the part of God in the book of Esther add to the controversy?

   _____

5. When God is silent, there are still accurate ways to determine right and wrong. Let's consider some passages on this subject so that you will be better equipped to interpret Esther. Meditate on the passage, and then answer the question.

A. *Trust in the Lord with all your heart, and lean not on your own understanding.*
(Proverbs 3:5 NKJV)

What does this verse say to do and not to do? Why, do you think?

_____

_____

B. *In those days there was no king in Israel; everyone did what was right in his own eyes.*
(Judges 21:25 NKJV)

This verse closes a description of one of the most decadent times in history. What was the problem with their measure of right and wrong?

_____

_____

C. *When the sentence for a crime is not quickly carried out, the hearts of the people are filled with schemes to do wrong.* (Ecclesiastes 8:11)

Why is a lack of immediate judgment an inaccurate measure of God's displeasure?

_____

_____

D. *A man cannot be established through wickedness.* (Proverbs 12:3a)

Why, according to the above, should we not do wrong things to get right results?

_____

_____

E. *I tell you, my friends, do not be afraid of those who kill the body and after that can do no more. But I will show you whom you should fear: Fear him who, after the killing of the body, has power to throw you into hell. Yes, I tell you, fear him.* (Luke 12:4–5)

Why should we not allow our fear of man to cause us to deny God, even if man can take our lives?

_____

_____

F. *Blessed are they whose ways are blameless, who walk according to the law of the Lord.*
(Psalm 119:1)

What standard will accurately show us right and wrong? What makes this standard more reliable than our own hearts?

_____

_____

6. Using the verses in question 5, or other verses, comment on the following statements concerning the choices of Mordecai and Esther.

   A. If Esther had not committed sexual immorality, then she would not have been queen, and she would not have been able to deliver her people from a holocaust. Therefore, she was right to participate in the contest.

   _____

   B. Mordecai and Esther did not have a choice. If they had refused, they might have lost their lives.

   _____

   C. If God had been displeased with Mordecai's or Esther's choices, He would have intervened and stopped them.

   _____

   D. God did not lead Esther into this contest, for His Word says to refrain from sexual immorality. However, His Word also says that He can bring beauty out of ashes.

   _____

   _____

Though we believe Esther and Mordecai may have been ruled by fear, how can we *not* be sympathetic? It seems the evidence is there that Mordecai loved Esther, and undoubtedly he feared for her life. Esther was alone, vulnerable, and probably quite young. She obeyed Mordecai, as she had always done growing up. We cannot know, for certain, *why* the two of them made such choices. John MacArthur states, "This issue must ultimately be resolved by God since He alone knows human hearts."[7]

7. Give an example of how we can have compassion for an individual who has made a wrong choice and yet not endorse that choice. Be specific about how you would show compassion to him or her without endorsing the wrong choice.

   _____

   _____

_____

_____

Continue learning your memory verse.

Day 3

THE SINS OF OUR FATHERS
AND THE GRACE OF GOD

(Dee) It is vital that we look at Scripture carefully before we try to interpret it. Often wrong interpretations are made when we assume we know what the passage says, or look at it very quickly. We can be like the diver who fails to measure the depth of a lake before he dives in. Observe the verses carefully. Often other Scriptures will shed light on a passage or on the historical context. I've cringed upon hearing some of the advice given to young women based on a flippant look at Esther.

Understanding the decadent practice of polygamy sheds light. Polygamy was never God's plan. God's plan was for one man and one woman to become one, in the holy estate of marriage. Polygamy was a result of sin. The first polygamist was Cain's descendant Lamech. (Lamech "took wives for himself," a phrase used repeatedly with polygamy. The phrase implies force, which you can see in Esther.) Lamech was also, like Cain, a murderer, and sang songs about his decadence to his wives (Genesis 4:19–24).

There is another fascinating passage early in Genesis describing the foundations of polygamy. Genesis 6 reports that evil "giants" took *all* the wives they chose. There are several interpretations for this passage. One suggests these giants were fallen angels, but angels were not sexual beings. Jesus says they do not marry. The interpretation that seems to fit the best with the rest of Scripture is that these "giants" were evil, tyrannical men.[8]

"Giants" in Scripture are not "fairytale" giants, but powerful and evil men, like Germany's Hitler or Cambodia's Pol Pot. In biblical days, "giants," or "mighty men," found polygamy an effective means of propagating their seed and their power. This same pattern seems to be happening with Xerxes and the horrific scene in which women "were taken" from all of his 120 provinces in Persia. There were also good kings who adopted the decadent cultural practice of polygamy, like David, but this was never pleasing to God. When David "took" Bathsheba, the heart of God was grieved. Polygamy has always been a terrible abuse of women, rooted in the lusts warned against in 1 John 2:15–17.

Not only is it helpful to understand the sin of polygamy, but it is also helpful to go back three generations before Esther to see what was happening with God's people.

8. Read Esther 2:5–6. How is Mordecai identified? How many generations had it been since his ancestor Kish had been taken captive from Jerusalem into this land by Nebuchadnezzar?

_____

Often the sins that bind us are generational sins. Breaking free means understanding the power of the past over our lives. In Esther's case, _three_ generations before these events occurred, we can see that the faith of key individuals in that generation was strong. Along with Mordecai's great-grandfather Kish were Daniel and his three young friends, whom we have come to know as Shadrach, Meshach, and Abednego.

9. Describe the choice that was made in each case. How were their choices different from those of the believers in the book of Esther?

A. Daniel 1:8–16 _____

_____

B. Daniel 3 (note particularly their response to the king in verses 17–18).

_____

_____

_____

"THE FIERY FURNACE FAILS"
JAMES TISSOT (1836–1902)

C. Daniel 6 _____

_____

_____

"Daniel in the Den
of Lions"
Briton Riviere (1840–1920)

D. As you meditate on the above painting by Riviere, what do you see?

_____

_____

Fifty years before Esther, Cyrus released the Jews from captivity, giving believers the freedom to return to the Holy Land. Many left, but some chose to stay. Did they stay in order to be missionaries in this pagan land? Again, this is controversial, but there are no records of an impact being made. It seems the believers had become comfortable, conformed to their surroundings and unconcerned about returning to their people. Commentator John Brug says that the book of Esther is deliberately written in the style of a Persian secular narrative to reflect the conditions and attitudes of Jews scattered in Persia in contrast to those of dedicated Jews in the Holy Land.[9]

John tells us, "love not the world." But the immediate ancestors of Esther and Mordecai seemed to have been conformed to the world around them, and they handed this empty way of life down to the next generation. So it is not surprising that the believers in Esther, in the beginning, instead of being vibrant, were reflecting the faded colors of their immediate ancestors.

Often strengths or weaknesses in our character can be traced back through several generations. The sins of fathers *are* passed on from generation to generation unless someone can have the kind of faith needed to break the chain.

10. As you look back over your "family tree," do you see any patterns that should be a warning to you? What strategy might you apply to break the chain? (You don't need to share this in the group.)

_____

_____

No matter what you have been handed from your past, no matter how you have failed, God is still eager to bestow His grace on you. The real hero in the book of Esther is God, and though His name is not mentioned, His hand is everywhere. He was with Esther in the midst of her distress and showed her grace. There is an important covenant word that appears in Esther 2:17. In the NIV it is translated "favor." In the Hebrew it is *hesed*. This is often translated "unfailing mercy" and indicates God's grace.

11. How do you see God preparing favor for Mordecai with Xerxes in Esther 2:19–23?

_____

12. What does it mean to you that God was with Esther and Mordecai in the above circumstances?

_____

_____

Review your memory passage.

Day 4

PRIDE HIDES THE COLORS OF HIS LOVE

Mordecai and Esther seemed to be operating on the basis of the fear of man, and that hid the colors of God's love. Another sin that always blocks His beauty is pride. No matter how lovely a person may be inside, when pride rules her heart, that haughty attitude is all that others can see.

(Dee) After my sister Sally and I became Christians, we began to share our faith with our sister Bonnie. Her defenses were always up because her siblings were "born again." Sometimes during my discussions with her, she would bring up controversial issues. She felt Christians were closed-minded and arrogant. Instead of listening to Bonnie and just letting her air her opinions, I would be argumentative, bringing her stereotypes to life. I was a bit haughty, to say the least. Solomon says, "Pride leads to arguments" (Proverbs 13:10a TLB).

How vital it is to keep talking to God about ourselves. It allows God a say when you dialogue with Him, asking Him questions like: *How do You feel about my relationship with this person?*

I remember praying and asking Him: *What is the wall I see Bonnie putting up toward You? Why does she seem so closed?*

Much to my surprise, God's Spirit told me the answer.

You guessed it. *I* was the wall. She couldn't see God over my own arrogance and agenda. I was a large part of the reason Bonnie wasn't considering Jesus seriously.

Genuinely broken, I went to Bonnie and said: "I've been obnoxious. I haven't listened to you about things that are really important to you. Please forgive me, Bonnie. I promise you, you are going to see a different sister."

For the next few years I was very conscious of showing her the love of Christ. The wall between us began to crumble. You see, I really love my sister, it's just that my pride, like the chlorophyll, hid the beautiful colors that He wanted to display before her.

The gospel can be so attractive, but how often we make it unattractive because we get in the way of the good news. As I humbled myself, as I died to my pride, God's colorful love began to show through me, and I could sense that Bonnie's heart was growing tender. I knew she was more inquisitive about my faith. One summer she said, "Dee, I've never heard you speak. Are you going to be anywhere near Utah this year?" Bonnie flew to Idaho to hear me speak that following February. When I asked if anyone wanted to know Jesus, I saw my sister's hand go up. You can only imagine how I felt.

(Kathy) I had a similar experience of dying to pride when I committed my life to Jesus. I was involved with a group that was planning a day for us to do some "street ministry" out in Southampton on Long Island. Though I love that area, that day I was dreading stepping out of the car. Some of my friends were eager to talk to people, but I felt paralyzed.

Certain people have the gift of being able to hand out tracts, or to just walk up to people they've never met and engage them in a conversation about God. But we are not all poured through the same mold. Paul shared the gospel in a way that was different from John's way, Mark's way, or Stephen's way. But no matter how we communicate God's love, we all need to approach people respectfully, being full of His compassion for them. This is where I failed, for instead of being really sensitive, I decided to "just go for it." I went up to two young women in their late twenties or early thirties sitting on a bench. I said something like: "Do you guys know Jesus?"

One of them immediately responded with anger in her eyes and sharpness in her tone:

> *You know what? You people are all the same. You just get in everyone's face with your agendas. You think everybody is supposed to believe what you believe. Why don't you do something else with your time?*

Her abrasiveness startled me. I could hardly move. I must have looked like a deer caught in headlights. I found myself staring at her with my mouth open . . . and it must have been God's grace, because I just started to weep. Then I plopped myself next to them and let out the biggest sigh.

> *Hey listen . . . I'm feeling so stupid. I'm sorry. This isn't me. This isn't my style. I've got to tell you, I used to think the same way you do about Christians. That's why I had trouble even going with my group today.*
> *I'm uncomfortable because I know I don't know you and you don't know me. I've just recently come to know who Jesus really is, and I just want others to know Him because He's wonderful.*

As soon as I humbled myself and spoke my true heart, there was a huge change in the two girls. Their countenances softened as we talked. We each shared about our lives. By the time I got up they said they were interested in visiting my church. We hugged good-bye.

When we are willing to die to our pride, to our agenda, and to humble ourselves by being honest, then glorious colors, like the colors of autumn leaves, can come forth. People will come to God, friendships will be cemented, marriages will thrive, joy will bubble up, and peace will flow. No wonder John tells us to die to "the pride of life." Pride is fleeting and gives a momentary exultation, but then all comes crashing down. With humility come honor, wisdom, and the things that can never pass away.

The next controversy in the book of Esther concerns Mordecai and his attitude toward Haman, the government official who was the right-hand man to the king. Again, be sure to read this passage carefully, for it may have been interpreted for you in a certain way, but try to come to it as if you were looking at it for the first time. Ask God to open your eyes.

It is important to know there was an ancient feud between the Jews and the Agagites. As you read the book of Esther, you will note that often Haman is referred to as "Haman the Agagite," and Mordecai as "Mordecai the Jew." Though the book of Esther is told with great subtlety, the author seems to be accentuating this difference between the men.

Read Esther 3 as an overview.

13. Describe how either Haman or Mordecai is described in the following passages:

    A. Esther 3:1_____

    B. Esther 3:10_____

    C. Esther 5:13_____

14. Should Mordecai have bowed to Haman or not? What do you learn from the following passages?

    A. Romans 13:1–2_____

    B. 1 Samuel 24:8_____

    C. 2 Samuel 14:4_____

15. Read Esther 3 again.

    A. Describe both of Mordecai's actions in verse 2. What do you think his motivation was?

    _____

    _____

    B. How did Haman react (vv. 5–6)?

    _____

In the *Word Biblical Commentary*, Frederic Bush notes that Jews regularly bowed to kings and those in authority. Then he comments on the reactions of both Mordecai and Haman:

> *The only thing in the context that makes both these reactions reasonable is the subtle allusion to the ancient tribal enmity between Jews and Amalekites. Mordecai's action is one of ethnic pride. He simply would not bow down to a descendant of the Amalekites (cf. Deut. 25:17–19). Haman's reaction is unmistakably motivated by a hatred so callous and senseless that, beside it, Mordecai's pride pales to insignificance.*[10]

C. Find the truth, the half-truth, and the lie in Haman's presentation to Xerxes (v. 8).

_____

_____

_____

D. Describe the edict (v. 13).

_____

_____

E. Describe the hearts of Haman and Xerxes (v. 15).

_____

Remember how John's letter continually contrasts a child of God and a child of Satan. Commentator John Whitcomb makes the point that "the titanic death-struggle of the book of Esther simply cannot be understood apart from the satanic purposes toward Israel."[11]

F. In what ways is Haman an illustration of 1 John 3:7–10?

_____

_____

16. Though Mordecai's sin paled in the face of Haman's, it still grieved the heart of God and hid the beauty of God. Think of a time recently when the pride of life did that in you—when you hesitated to admit you were wrong, or spoke unkind words, or exaggerated to make yourself look better. (You don't have to share this in the group.) In that situation, how was it "not easy being green"?

_____

_____

If you know the following praise chorus, sing it with all your heart and soul and mind as a private prayer to the Lord. If you don't know it, you might want to meditate on it as a prayer.

Breathe on me, Breath of God, fill me with life anew
That I may love what Thou dost love, and do what Thou wouldst do

Breathe on me, Breath of God, till I am wholly Thine,
Until this earthly part of me glows with Thy fire divine.
(Public Domain)

Day 5

ESTHER AND THE WIZARD OF OZ

One of our favorite movies is *The Wizard of Oz*. Every once in a while we'll watch the video of this wonderful story of friendships in a magical land. Remember how it begins in black and white? Dorothy is at her Auntie Em's in Kansas, and the farm, the landscape, and life itself seem dreary. Dorothy longs for a more exciting life in a land "Somewhere Over the Rainbow."

A tornado suddenly sends the house and Dorothy swirling. Hitting her head, she begins to dream, and suddenly she and Toto are in the colorful Land of Oz. The dull blacks and whites disappear. Dorothy skips down a yellow brick road toward an emerald castle. An evil witch with a shocking green face appears. A good witch gives Dorothy a pair of ruby red slippers. What a change from Auntie Em's farm in Kansas! All this is symbolized by a transformation to Technicolor.

If we were to make a movie of the book of Esther, we would use a similar technique. In the beginning of this book the central characters, Esther and her guardian, Mordecai, who are Jews, seem to be operating on the basis of arrogance and fear. Instead of aligning themselves with God, they hide their colors of faith. Mordecai also engages in a prideful dispute with the king's right-hand man, Haman. Instead of being vibrant with the life of God, Mordecai and Esther are faded. Instead of shining like stars amidst a crooked and perverse generation, they act like chameleons, those ugly little lizards that take on the dull grays, greens, or browns of their background, so that no one will notice them. Yet later in the book, when faced with an edict for a holocaust against Jews, there is a change. Instead of pride, there is sackcloth and ashes. Instead of fear, there is courage. Instead of being conformed to their world, they are transformed by the truth of God. Instead of clinging to their lives, they are willing to lay them down. This is when we would symbolize the wonderful transformation in God's people by turning the movie from black and white to Technicolor.

Review your memory passage. Read Esther 4 as an overview.

17. As you review the opening three chapters of Esther, consider how well Mordecai and Esther did in living up to the following principles in 1 John. Describe first the principle, or "the clothing" a child of God should put on, and then describe how well either Mordecai or Esther wore that clothing.

A. 1 John 1:7 _____

_____

B. 1 John 2:10–11 _____

_____

C. 1 John 2:15–17 _____

_____

D. 1 John 3:7 _____

_____

E. 1 John 3:16 _____

_____

F. 1 John 4:18 _____

_____

18. Describe the "clothing" Mordecai puts on in Esther 4:1–3. What change does this indicate?

_____

_____

19. Describe the "clothing" Esther puts on in Esther 4:15–16. What change does this indicate?

_____

_____

20. Share a time when you or someone close to you humbled himself. What was done and said? What was the result?

_____

_____

21. Why is it so hard to die to pride, do you think? Where is God asking you to die to pride?

_____

_____

Sometimes our group prayer times lack authenticity because of pride. Seldom do we request prayer for our battles with sin. Because of pride and the fear of man, we're hesitant to admit where we are struggling. Yet if we die to these things, not only can we get help from our sisters, but we provide a model of living in the light to them. Determine this week to share, either in your small group or with a trusted brother or sister, an area where you really need both prayer and accountability.

22. What stood out to you this week? How will you apply it to your life?

_____

_____

PRAYER TIME

Lift up an area of need in your life and allow the women to support you in prayer. (Prayers can be short and simple—even "I agree, Lord.")

CLOTHED IN TRUTH:

Week 8: TRUE BLUE

"Then you will know the truth, and the truth will set you free."
(JOHN 8:32)

TRUE BLUE

(Dee)

Since we are just a short drive from Colorado, family vacations have often been ski trips. We have loved skiing through the silent snow, breathing in the crisp mountain air, and beholding the beauty of our Creator's handiwork: majestic mountains, towering green pines, and a backdrop of the bluest of skies.

The spirit of truth is like that fresh mountain air, breeding freedom and life, whereas the spirit of falsehood is like the smog of a city, breeding bondage and death. How I want to be a woman who is like that clear blue sky, discerning, embracing, and proclaiming the truth. I have learned to seek out friends like that as well, women who are so filled with truth that out of the overflow of their hearts, their words and actions continually spur me to greater heights.

Believers like this are rare gems, and when I discover one, I pursue her in friendship. It's the reason I was drawn to Kathy. I love going over the Word of God with Kathy not only because of her depth, but also because of her honesty. Often she says the things many of us are thinking but are hesitant to articulate. For example, when I showed her the "blacks and whites" of 1 John, she said:

> What?! *These verses make me want to run for the hills!*
> *Is John saying that if I don't always do what is right, I'm not a child of God?*

Likewise, when we went over the dark passage in Esther concerning the "beauty" contest, she said:

> *Dee, why didn't I see this before? Esther slept with the king! Why don't we hear more about this?*

God loves it when we ask questions of Him. He pleads, "Come now, let us reason together" (Isaiah 1:18a). He knows what we are thinking—we might as well tell Him! If your group is going to be vital and growing, be honest with one another—with your questions and with your struggles with sin. Don't pretend to be what you are not, or your pretending is like a smog settling over the group. When we are truthful, as hard as it is (and it is!), we become like the mountain air, breathing love, freedom, and life over one another.

(Kathy) My mother used to always say, "You are who you are around." There was a time in my life when I would roll my eyes at some of her tidbits of motherly wisdom. But most of us,

as we get older, realize that Mom and Dad weren't so dumb. It's true: "You are who you are around." Just as friends who are filled with truth revive you, those who are apathetic pull you down. I see it all the time now. I see it with some of my friends. They may think that the friends they have chosen don't influence them, but they do. I've seen people who were once filled with zeal and a hunger and thirst for righteousness become complacent. They've grown apathetic toward the things that used to stir their souls toward holiness.

As John turns to the subject of truth and falsehood, we see how important it is to surround ourselves with those filled with truth and to beware of those who could lead us astray. John's writings have been compared to a piece of music. He begins with a theme and then builds. We've seen him do it with light and darkness and love and hate. Now he does it with truth and falsehood.

He begins with the ultimate lie and then builds. There was a specific problem of "brothers" who were not really brothers at all, leaving the church and spreading lies. They were polluting the health of the body. John, concerned for his flock, speaks forcefully, beginning with the ultimate lie. However, it is *vital* to understand that the application is not just to false teachers and cult members, but also to a whole "spirit of antichrist" at work in the world, a spirit that pervades our world today. You read its philosophy in women's magazines, hear it on talk shows, and see it in the lifestyles of those who are apathetic toward the things of God. These people may even claim to know God, but it is important to watch for the red flags John now gives us.

VIDEO NOTES FOR WEEK 8
TRUE BLUE

Thoughts I want to remember:

_____

_____

_____

THE BOOK OF ESTHER SHOWS US THE SPIRIT OF THE ANTICHRIST
1. FRIENDS INFLUENCE US

You are who you are _____.

Bad company corrupts _____ *character.* (1 Corinthians 15:33b)

Haman influenced Xerxes. Like his father, Satan, Haman practices deceit. He tells:

    a truth

    a half-_____

    and an outright _____

       . . . it is not in the king's best interest to t_____ them. (Esther 3:8c)

Whoever touches you touches the _____ of his eye. (Zechariah 2:8b)

2. The Spirit of Antichrist

John explains that the Antichrist is coming, but before he comes, there is a _____ of anti_____ at work in the world.

It's not just in the cult member who knocks at your door. This spirit is every_____.

3. Four Red Flags for the Counterfeit

A. The ultimate lie: *Who is the liar? It is the man who denies that*

J_____ *is the* C_____. (1 John 2:22)

The ultimate lie denies the atonement and the true i_____ of Jesus.

B. A second red flag is raised when they leave the body of believers.

They went out from us, but they did not really belong to us. For if they had belonged to us, they would have r_____ with us; but their going showed that none of them b_____ to us. (1 John 2:19)

C. A third red flag is the claim that His Spirit led them contrary to His W_____.

D. A fourth red flag is agreement with the world.

They are from the world and therefore speak from the _____ of the world, and the world _____ to them. (1 John 4:5)

Icebreaker *(Hear from several women for each question.)*

1. Think about a friend who is like the clear mountain air—so filled with truth and the desire to walk in the truth that being with her revives you. Share something about her.

_____

2. What stood out to you in the video? Why?

_____

_____

YOU ARE WHO YOU ARE AROUND

John has been talking about lies and liars from the beginning of his letter. Up until now he has been telling us to take note of *behavior*.

Prepare your heart for study by singing songs to the Lord in your time alone with Him, either songs from Appendix B or ones you know.

1. Review the behavioral warning flags for the counterfeit:

   A. 1 John 1:6_____

   B. 1 John 2:4_____

   C. 1 John 2:9_____

   D. 1 John 2:15_____

Now, beginning in 1 John 2:18, the apostle looks at *doctrinal* warning flags for the counterfeit. He tells us how to discern the difference between the spirit of falsehood and the spirit of truth. Though the world cares nothing for doctrine and measures a Christian's authenticity only on the basis of love, we, as believers, must consider doctrine as well. We must consider the things we hear and measure them against God's plumb line of truth. Even a small deception can distort truth, like a dab of black paint distorts a pint of bold red or bright yellow. What was once pure and lovely is ruined. So it is with the spirit of falsehood.

John explains that the Antichrist, the one who will war against Christ, is coming. *Before* he comes, his way is being prepared by "many antichrists," or, as theologian John Stott explains, "a spirit of antichrist at work in the world."[1] We will look at this spirit closely tomorrow, for it is not just in cults. It pervades our culture.

Read 1 John 2:18–27 carefully as an overview.

2. According to 1 John 2:18, who is coming, and who will precede him?

   _____

3. What is one sign, according to 1 John 2:19, of the counterfeit?

   _____

Leaving the fellowship of believers is one of the ways we recognize the cults. Historically, cults have formed when a charismatic leader arose within the ranks of Christianity claiming a special vision or knowledge with a "new and improved" interpretation of classic Christianity. When he left, he took many with him. This new group may call themselves Christian, but they are an exclusive group, and they refuse to fellowship with those who do not hold to their unique interpretation of Scripture. "Withdrawing," John says, is evidence that they never really belonged.

It is also true that "believers" who leave the church because they are "disillusioned with the institutionalized church" and prefer to worship God on their own are falling into error. Though it *is* true we can and should worship God anywhere, we absolutely need the body of believers. The institutionalized church does, indeed, have many flaws, for it is made up of sinners, but there *are* healthy churches holding to the Word of God and demonstrating love for one another. If your church is unhealthy, find a healthy one! It is not just important but vital that we each be an active part of a local church. "We are who we are around."

(Kathy) There are people who have dropped out of the church and out of the fellowship of believers. Subtly and slowly they are uncomfortable with holy and sacred talk. It's like the progression in Psalm 1, from standing in the way of sinners to finally sitting in the seat of mockers, mocking the things of God. The goal for living becomes more of a "let's not hurt anyone," "let's try to be good people," and "let's not judge anybody." I believe that kind of mentality sets in because the person no longer wants to be under the gaze of God Himself. Because when you allow God to look at you, He will judge you rightly, see you correctly, and challenge you to die so you can live. Where you once received the call to holiness, you now just let the phone keep ringing or pick it up and quickly hang up.

(Dee) Steve and I had a period in our lives when our local church became very unhealthy. After trying to be part of a change for health, after failing miserably, and after seeking God diligently, we *did* leave, but we didn't just drop out of the body of believers. We found a healthy church and joined. Being part of a local church keeps you accountable. Each of us needs to be under the protection and the authority of a local church where we are continually challenged to walk in the truth of the Word of God.

4. How has being part of a local church helped you to grow? What are some signs of a healthy church? (A healthy church is made up of healthy believers, so the four principles of 1 John should be seen. First John 2:12–14 describes a few things you should see.)

_____

_____

The *Word Biblical Commentary* explains that it is quite possible the heretics who had left the early church, "who had withdrawn from the congregation, had been claiming a special source of 'knowledge' as the basis for their theological stance."[2] Therefore, John now reminds the believers that they already have the two things they need to know the truth, and they do not need a "special source" of knowledge.

5. Of what does John remind the believers in 1 John 2:20?

_____

6. Our anointing comes from the Holy Spirit, who is called "the Spirit of truth" (John 14:17). What else do you learn about Him from the following?

A. 1 John 2:21b_____

B. 1 John 2:27_____

_____

John is not saying that we should not listen to other believers, or that we cannot have teachers, for he himself is teaching. He is saying that our primary teacher is the Holy Spirit. We can read the Scriptures on our own, and He will illumine us. We can trust Him to guide us into truth.

7. In addition to the Holy Spirit, what is our other source of truth? (See 1 John 2:14b, 24.)

_____

(Dee) The Holy Spirit and the Word both give the truth of God; therefore, they will always be in agreement. It amazes me when I hear people say that God led them to marry an unbeliever or to have an abortion. In the movie *The Apostle*, the senior pastor's wife justifies her sexual immorality by telling her husband that God led her to leave him and to take up with the youth pastor. Astonished, he asks simply, *"Our God?"*

God gets blamed for a lot, but His Spirit never leads against His Word. A huge red flag is raised when someone claims God led them to do something that contradicts His Word. These heretics in the early church were doing that, and John says that goes against all reason!

8. Paul uses even stronger language in Galatians 1:6–9. What does he say?

_____

_____

9. Give an example of how you would know that the Spirit was *not* leading because there was a conflict with the Word of God.

_____

Begin learning your memory verse.

THE SPIRIT OF ANTICHRIST

It is vital to realize that "the spirit of the antichrist" does not *just* show up with the cult member who occasionally knocks on our doors. The spirit of the antichrist truly *reigns* in our world today. It's in our movies, our television shows, our universities, our women's magazines, and in the minds and mouths of those who do not know God. It flows right into our homes through the river of the mass media. It tries to pollute our hearts through the mouths of well-intentioned but misguided counselors, teachers, and even ministers—and we must be able to recognize it.

How do we recognize this foolish spirit so it doesn't pollute our own hearts and souls? John begins with the primary test. Understanding this test can help you spot the spirit of falsehood when you watch a talk show, read an editorial, or listen to your brother-in-law philosophize at Thanksgiving.

10. Find the ultimate lie in 1 John 2:22b.

_____

_____

Jesus means "Jehovah saves" or "Savior." *Christ* means "the anointed one, the Messiah." *Therefore, the one who denies that Jesus is the Christ is denying the atonement for sin and the true identity of Jesus.* This spirit may call Jesus a teacher or a prophet, but it does not believe He is fully man and fully God. It preaches a different Jesus. Those controlled by this spirit may admit that the world has problems, but the solution of the Scriptures (repentance and faith in Christ) is foolishness to them. Instead they suggest education, money, or "spirituality," but not Christianity. (Doesn't *that* make for much more pleasant dinner conversation?) They trust in themselves or their own way of defining God, but not in the living Christ.

11. Name some places you have seen or heard this "spirit of antichrist."

_____

_____

Jennifer, a young woman who was trying to overcome a painful past, was going to a woman who claimed to be a Christian counselor. But during one session this counselor told Jennifer that there were many ways to God, and Jesus was just one of those ways. Reflectively, Jennifer said,

> *Though I loved this woman, at that moment I recognized the deception in what I was hearing. I thought,* If that were true, why was the Cross necessary? And what about the verse that tells us there is no other name under heaven by which we may be saved? *I realized I had been told the "ultimate lie," and I knew I had to change counselors. Only the truth could set me free.*

12. This spirit of antichrist not only denies the deity of Christ, it may also deny the humanity of Christ. John addresses this later in his letter, and again, in his second letter. Record everything you can discover about the spirit of the antichrist from the following passages.

A. 1 John 4:1–3 _____

_____

_____

B. 2 John 7 _____

_____

Just as denying the Deity of Christ is a lie, so is denying the humanity of Christ. It might *seem* like it is honoring Jesus to de-emphasize His humanity, but it is dishonoring. He was fully man and fully God. He experienced temptation, as we do, and He is therefore able to sympathize with our weaknesses and help us (Hebrews 2:18). Those who minimize His humanity often are reluctant to come to Him as an intercessor but look for a different intercessor whom they feel will better understand their humanity. The same lie that plagued the early Christians is prevalent within our ranks today.

13. Of what does John remind us in 1 John 4:4?

_____

_____

In your personal quiet time, you may wish to sing the following praise chorus:

Greater is He that is in me
Greater is He that is in me
Greater is He that is in me
Than he that is in the world

Words and Music by Lanny Wolfe ©1973 Lanny Wolfe Music Co. All Rights Reserved. Used by Permission.

Continue learning your memory passage.

Day 3

IT SPEAKS FROM THE VIEWPOINT OF THE WORLD

Remember how John has said that either your Father is God or your father is Satan? In the following passage, note the repeated words: "are from." (Some translations say "are of.") John wants us to see the source behind everything we hear.

14. Read 1 John 4:4–6 and identify:

Who is John talking about?　*Where are they from?*　*What characterizes them?*

v. 4_____　_____　_____

v. 5_____　_____　_____

v. 6_____　_____　_____

15. How would you summarize the test in this passage for differentiating the Spirit of truth from the spirit of falsehood?

_____

_____

16. This spirit was at work in the days of ancient Persia, in the story of Esther. It embraced many ideas, but turned its back on the truth of the God of Israel. The solutions that the Persian leaders sought were from the world. Remember the false values that John warns against in 1 John 2:15–17? As a review of Esther, see if you can find examples of each of these values in the opening two chapters. Give verse references that exemplify these worldly values in Xerxes, his counselors, or Haman:

A. The lust of the flesh (bodily appetites) _____

_____

_____

B. The lust of the eyes (greed and the ostentatious display of wealth)_____

_____

_____

C. The pride of life (power, popularity, position)_____

_____

_____

17. The spirit of falsehood tolerates all opinions except one. It embraces everything the world believes but rejects the truth of Jesus. It shows tolerance toward all people but rejects those who follow the one true God. How do you see this in Esther 3:8?

_____

_____

Today this same spirit of falsehood ironically *preaches* tolerance, yet does not *practice* tolerance toward Christians. It ridicules the viewpoint of the believer in politics, in education, and even in religion. It is the spirit of the antichrist. It listens to every viewpoint except one, and seeks to annihilate *that* viewpoint. And the world listens to that viewpoint, repeating its slogans as if they were the gospel truth. It labels us as "right-wing zealots," "fundamentalist fanatics," or "narrow-minded bigots," hoping to persuade others not to tolerate us. The origin of this spirit is of old. It is our ancient foe.

18. John tells us that the world listens to this false spirit. How do you see this in Esther 3:9-11?

_____

_____

Though it may appear in this passage as if Xerxes refuses Haman's monetary bribe, he does not. What was happening was a common form of Oriental bargaining to help Xerxes save face. Xerxes was saying, "Oh no, that's too much—keep your money," but then Mordecai persisted, and finally, Xerxes took it. The evidence that Xerxes eventually took the money is found in Esther 4:7 and in Esther's statement: "I and my people have been *sold* . . ." (Esther 7:4a, emphasis added).

Before the crisis in the book of Esther, the believers (the Jews) had been walking in the ways of the world. It was difficult to tell the difference between them and the citizens of Persia. But the king's edict for their extermination brought them to their knees and to their senses. They repented, they put on sackcloth and ashes, they fasted and, we assume therefore, that they prayed, crying out to God for wisdom and truth. Here is where it becomes very clear that though they had hidden their light, they were, indeed, from God.

19. Read Esther 4 as an overview.

A. Review Mordecai's actions and attitude in Esther 4:1–2.

_____

B. Describe the attitude of God's people in every province (Esther 4:3).

_____

C. Describe Esther's attitude and action in Esther 4:4–5.

_____

D. List all the information that Hathach gave to Esther in Esther 4:7–9.

_____

_____

E. What is Esther's initial response? What were her fears (Esther 4:10–11)?

_____

_____

F. If you had been in Esther's place, how might you have felt? Why?

_____

_____

If you just took Esther at face value and didn't realize the severity of the big picture, you might think,

You know what, Esther? You're exactly right. That all makes sense. You shouldn't go.

Each of us faces times in our lives when, if we have eternity in mind, there is a glaring choice to be made between the path of God and the path of the world. Yet, filled with fear, we rationalize. We dance around to save our own skin. We might not come clean in situations where we have hurt someone; we'll water down our convictions so that we don't look like a "closed-minded Christian"; we'll compromise on the job so that we might be promoted; or we'll fail to speak the truth in love to a friend so that we don't offend, to the detriment of their spiritual health.

20. Is there an area in your life where you need to make a hard choice and walk in the truth or speak the truth? What is it? (You don't need to share this in the group.)

_____

_____

Review your memory passage.

TRUE BLUE

Mordecai didn't let Esther off the hook. Instead, he awakened her and made the most famous speech in the book of Esther. He gave her three reasons for doing what was *right*, even though he realized it might mean her death. But these reasons were so filled with truth that her former rationale no longer had a say. Today we will look carefully at the three reasons Mordecai gave her for "dying to herself." Then we will look at her response. Read Esther 4:12–17 carefully.

21. What is the first reason Mordecai gives in Esther 4:13? What is he telling her?

_____

Esther cannot hide anymore. Mordecai had already revealed his identity, and many knew she was linked to him. Trying to cling to her life at this point was futile. Do you see the parallel? Jesus said:

> *If you cling to your life, you will lose it; but if you give it up for me, you will save it.* (Matthew 10:39 TLB)

If we are willing to die for what is important to God, there *will* be new life. Not only that, there will be a sense of wellness. Kathy writes in her song "A Different Road":

> *Don't want to live without the peace*
> *that comes to me when I am by Your side*
> *I've known the freedom there*
> *can't find it anywhere*
> *but in Christ Jesus*

The world passes away, but the person who lives for God stores up treasures that can never pass away.

22. What is Mordecai's next argument in Esther 4:14a?

_____

_____

What Mordecai knew, as every Jew knew, was that God's people were the apple of His eye, and He would *always* have a remnant. If Esther shrank from her responsibility, God would use someone else, somewhere else. The Jews in Persia would be wiped out, and God would move His anointing to someone else. This is sobering. No one is indispensable. It doesn't matter who you are or what you do. If you will *not* heed the call of God, He will most definitely use someone else. He is looking, the Scripture tells us, for those who are *fully* committed to Him:

> *For the eyes of the LORD range throughout the earth to strengthen those whose hearts are fully committed to him.* (2 Chronicles 16:9a)

If we are not committed to Him, He will find someone who is. That is Mordecai's point to Esther. Elizabeth Dole said that understanding this truth caused her to want to live a radically obedient life, so that He would use her and not move on to someone else.

23. How could you increase your faithfulness to the responsibilities God has given you?

_____

_____

24. Finally Mordecai gave the clincher, the most famous verse in Esther. What does he say in Esther 4:14b?

_____

Some might interpret the above verse to mean that God led Esther to sleep with the king so that she could one day deliver her people from a holocaust. We do not agree with that interpretation, for God's Spirit never leads against His Word. Since God's Word is clear that we are to refrain from sexual immorality, we know His Spirit did not lead Esther to commit sexual immorality.

However, it is also true that our God is a Master of bringing beauty out of ashes, and that He can redeem our failures. If we are honest about our weaknesses, then He can use us mightily.

25. When Jesus began His public ministry, He began by reading from the scroll of Isaiah. What are some of the changes our Redeemer has the power to make in our life, according to Isaiah 61:3?

_____

_____

26. In what areas of your life do you pray for Him to turn your ashes into beauty, or your mourning into praise?

_____

_____

27. What is your part in the above? What is God's part?

_____

28. What is Esther's response to the truth that Mordecai spoke to her (Esther 4:15–16)?

_____

_____

Esther truly provides a model for us. So often we as believers come up with a strategy and then ask God to bless it. Instead we should, as Esther models, seek God's strategy, and then it *will* be blessed!

29. In what ways can you see Esther now exemplifying the principles of 1 John?

_____

_____

Day 5

GOD ON THE MOVE

30. Describe the king's response to Esther in Esther 5:1–3.

_____

_____

ENGRAVING OF ESTHER THE QUEEN
L. CHERON, PAINTER; N. PARR, ENGRAVER (1762)

31. What does Esther tell Xerxes (Esther 5:4)? Why do you think she makes him wait?

_____

_____

32. During the interval in which Esther makes Xerxes wait (Esther 5:5 through 6:14), how do you see God on the move?

_____

_____

Again, Esther provides a wonderful model for us of waiting on God. We must be patient, trusting Him to work out problems that we have placed in His capable hands. Exodus 14:14 tells us, "The LORD will fight for you; you need only to be still." Many times we want to make a quick phone call, or send off an e-mail to get our point across, but if we would just wait, and pray, we would see God work in the hearts of the people involved. By the time Esther is ready to speak the truth, the king's heart has been prepared, like tilled soil, for the seed of God's truth.

33. Describe what happened in Esther 7.

_____

_____

"THE WRATH
OF AHASUERUS"
JAN STEEN (1626–1679)

34. This painting of Xerxes (also known as Ahasuerus) may have been inspired by Proverbs 19:12, which tells us that "a king's rage is like the roar of a lion." What do you see in this painting?

_____

(Dee) Do you remember the prayer group of mothers I told you about in the video? I am so thankful that Satan was unable to divide us, for when our daughters were seniors in high school, we saw God do amazing things through their friendship. They were asking God to show them how to reach their high school for Christ. At one point they decided to follow Esther's example and fast. Instead of a total three-day fast, they went without their lunches for a week. (In the video, Sally says, "We fasted for a week," but she meant "We fasted *lunches* for a week.")

At the end of the week they learned that Campus Crusade was bringing the *Jesus* movie to town the week before Easter. They wondered: *Would it be possible to have a private showing at the high school for teens?* Campus Crusade quickly agreed, but the challenge was to persuade their principal, whom they called "Dr. K." I remember when Sally told me their plan, I thought: *There is no way that is going to happen.* I'll always remember the conversation I had with Sally:

> "Mom, we're going to go without lunches for another week. Then we are going to draw straws. Whoever gets the shortest straw will go to Dr. K and ask if we can have a private showing, announce it over the loudspeaker system, and put the life-size posters of Jesus in the halls."
>
> "Honey, don't get your hopes up. I can't see how Dr. K will agree to this."
>
> "But Mom, don't you remember how God worked in the heart of Xerxes after Esther and her friends fasted?"
>
> "Yes, but . . ."
>
> "Mom, Dr. K is a much more reasonable man than Xerxes."
>
> "But this is a public high school—and they are so jittery about Jesus. Remember, the world tolerates everyone except Jesus."
>
> My lack of faith didn't slow down Sally or her friends. They continued their fast, excitement filling their hearts. On Friday they drew straws.
>
> Sally drew the shortest straw. She went to Dr. K and asked if she could have an appointment to speak to him about something important.
>
> "This is a good time for me, Sally. We can talk right now."
>
> Sally and her friends wanted to follow Esther's example of allowing God to move in their principal's heart, so Sally didn't want to tell him what she wanted right away.
>
> "I'd appreciate it so much if I could tell you next Monday, Dr. K."
>
> "What's this about, Sally?"
>
> "Sir, I would rather wait. Could we do it Monday?"
>
> He raised his eyebrows quizzically, but put her down for Monday at 8 A.M.

That weekend we saw God working behind the scenes. Both Sally and the principal's daughter, Katie, were in a high school singing group called "The Madrigals." On Saturday they were traveling to sing at an important concert for which they had prepared all year. Sally decided to go down the night before to see her brother (and shop for a prom dress!). However, in her rush, she forgot the medieval black evening gown that she needed for the Madrigal concert. She called Katie, who came to the rescue by asking her dad to unlock the choir room and get Sally's dress so they could bring it in the morning.

But the next morning it was snowing. Fearing Interstate 80 would be closed, Dr. K hurried Katie out, forgetting Sally's dress.

When Katie and Dr. K. arrived at the concert, Sally came running up, thanking them for bringing her dress. They both turned white. Dr. K said, "Oh, Sally! I can't believe it. I left it hanging on the hook."

Sally *did* sing, but she had to wear her green prom dress.

"I know everyone was waiting for the girl who stuck out like a green thumb to break out into a solo or a dance, but she never did. It was pretty embarrassing. I remember that Dr. K felt *so* badly."

That Monday, when Sally walked into Dr. K's office, he said: "Whatever you want, Sally, you can have it."

Life-size posters of *Jesus* were hung in the halls of the public high school. Fliers were placed on every car. Several hundred students came, and dozens gave their lives to Christ. The girls had Bible studies for beginners already set up, and the discipling process began.

If God is for us, who can be against us?

35. What have you learned from Esther that you can apply to your life?

_____

_____

PRAYER TIME

Cluster in small groups. Look over your answers to questions 23, 26, and 27. If you would be willing to lift up one of these in prayer, and then allow the other women to support you with prayer, do so now. You may want to close with "What a Friend We Have in Jesus."

PRINCIPLE FOUR:

CLOTHED IN MERCY:

Week 9: WHITE AS SNOW

"Have mercy on me, O God, according to your unfailing love; according to your great compassion. . . . Wash me, and I will be whiter than snow." (PSALM 51:1, 7B)

WHITE AS SNOW

Max Lucado helps us imagine the amazing day when Christ will come:

As if the sky were a curtain, the drapes of the atmosphere part. A brilliant light spills onto the earth. There are no shadows. None. From whence came the light begins to tumble a river of color—spiking crystals of every hue ever seen and a million more never seen. Riding on the flow is an endless fleet of angels. They pass through the curtains one myriad at a time until they occupy every square inch of the sky. North. South. East. West. Thousands of silvery wings rise and fall in unison, and over the sound of the trumpets, you can hear the cherubim and seraphim chanting, "Holy, holy, holy."

. . . Suddenly the heavens are quiet. All is quiet. The angels turn, you turn, the entire world turns—and there he is. Jesus.[1]

Most of us feel some discomfort at the thought of this moment, for we know He is holy and we are not. Yet, it is possible, according to John's letter, to prepare for this day. When Jesus sees you, wouldn't you love to see pleasure in His eyes? How can your wedding gown be as white as snow, and embroidered with gold? The refrain of 1 John has been to become like the Lord. How can the imprint be strong in you?

> *Light—Because He is light, we must stay in the light.*
> *Death—Because He laid down His life, we must die to ourselves.*
> *Truth—Because He is truth, we must live by the truth.*

And finally,

> *Mercy—Because He is merciful, we must be merciful.*

We encourage you to complete your homework, for in Day 5 there is an exciting culminating secret that can change your life.

VIDEO NOTES FOR WEEK 9
WHITE AS SNOW

Thoughts I want to remember:

_____

_____

_____

_____

_____

THREE ASPECTS OF MERCY SEEN IN GOD

1. G_____ for the brokenhearted

2. F_____ for the transgressor

3. G_____ toward those in need

REAL AND COUNTERFEIT CHRISTIANS

When we fail as Dee did, how can we *know* we are children of God? Our confidence *must* be in the mercy of Christ and not in ourselves.

And this is the testimony: God has given us eternal life, and this life is in his Son.

He who has the Son h_____ l_____; he who does not have the Son of

God d_____ n_____ have life. I write these things to you who believe in

the name of the Son of God so that you may k_____ that you have eternal life.
(1 John 5:11–13)

Yet there are counterfeit Christians. How can we know we are not one of them?
We must look at the desire of our hearts and the persistent direction of our life. If Jesus really lives within us, there will be a difference.

Dear children, let us not love with words or tongue but with a_____ and in truth. This

then is how we know that we b_____ to the truth, and how we set our hearts at r_____

in his presence whenever our hearts c_____ us. For G_____ is greater than our hearts,

and he knows everything. (1 John 3:18–20)

GOD WAS NOT A "LOVE-FORGETTER," AND WE MUST NOT BE EITHER

Xerxes and Esther show us the contrast between an unbeliever and a believer. After Xerxes saved the life of Esther, he forgot about his promise to the rest of her people. He was a "love-forgetter," but Esther was not. She went back, saying:

For how can I bear to see d_____ fall on my people?

How can I bear to see the destruction of my family? (Esther 8:6)

THIS IS THE PROMISE:

And so we know and rely on the love God has for us.

God is l_____. Whoever lives in love lives in God, and God in him.

In this way, love is made c_____ among us so that we will have confidence

on the day of judgment, because in this world we are like him. (1 John 4:16–17)

ICEBREAKER *(Hear from several women for each question.)*

1. Look at Rembrandt's painting *The Return of the Prodigal Son* below. Comment on one aspect of the painting. What does it mean to you? (Don't worry about repetition in the group for God uses repetition for emphasis.)

   _____

2. What stood out to you in the video? Why?

   _____

Day 1

GOD IS MERCY, SO WE MUST BE MERCIFUL

God is the father in the story of the prodigal son, the father who opens his arms to his erring child, the father who is willing to embrace the shame of a rebellious child, and who rejoices at his child's homecoming.

"THE RETURN OF THE PRODIGAL SON"
REMBRANDT (1606–1669)

(Dee) For so many years I have wandered through art museums with my art enthusiast husband and daughter, Sally. I have been the impatient one, wondering how they can stand *so* long in front of *one* painting. But a book titled *The Return of the Prodigal* by Henri Nouwen is changing me, slowing me down, helping me see. Nouwen reminisces about the first time he saw this painting, as a poster:

> *I could not take my eyes away. I felt drawn by the intimacy between the two figures, the warm red of the man's cloak, the golden yellow of the boy's tunic, and the mysterious light engulfing them both. But most of all it was the hands—the old man's hands—as they touched the boy's shoulders that reached me in a place where I had never been reached before.*[2]

How eager Nouwen was to go to St. Petersburg and see the original. It did not disappoint him. The first day he spent the whole afternoon in front of the masterpiece, making the museum guard a bit uneasy. He pulled up a chair. He took copious notes, observing each figure in the painting and how each related to the other—the colors, the light, the hands, the expressions. He observed the painting from different angles, watching how the light fell at noon, at midafternoon, and as evening approached. Nouwen's time with Rembrandt's masterpiece deepened his walk with God as nothing else had ever done.

When Nouwen first studied this painting, he identified with the sons—first the younger son, and then the elder son. That is what most of us do when we study this famous parable, for we have all been prodigals, like the younger son, wasting the gifts, time, and money God has given us. And we have all been ungrateful and jealous, like the elder son. Nouwen wrote, "It feels somehow good to be able to say: 'These sons are like me.' It gives a sense of being understood."[3] But how does it feel to identify with the father? This is the core, Nouwen says, of the teaching of Christ. This is the multifold secret of being embroidered with the colors of His love. This is the heart of 1 John. As Henri Nouwen stood gazing at Rembrandt's painting, he realized that the real questions we should be asking ourselves are:

> *Do I want to be like the father?*

> *Do I want to be not just the one forgiven but the one who forgives?*

> *Do I want to be not just the one welcomed home, but the one who welcomes home?*

> *Do I want to be not just the one who receives compassion, but offers it as well?*

So often the best-selling Christian books, the most treasured sermons, and the whole orientation of the church is about what Christianity can do for us. We are still intent on what the Father can do for us. Instead of being "like Him in this world" (1 John 4:17), it's still all about us. But our wedding gowns will never be embroidered with the colors of His love until we can love the way He does. The *final* principle John addresses is mercy, which is shown so clearly in the father in this parable. Nouwen says that the father's mercy consists of:

- Grief (for the brokenhearted)
- Forgiveness (for the transgressor)
- Generosity (for those in need)

1. Read Luke 15:11–32 and answer:
   A. Describe what happened with the younger son (vv. 15–24).

   _____

   _____

   B. Describe what happened with the older son (vv. 25–31).

   _____

   _____

   C. Describe the heart of the father, giving verse references to show:

   - Grief (for the brokenhearted)_____

   - Forgiveness (for the transgressor)_____

   - Generosity (for those in need)_____

Spend some time in prayer for yourself, that you will develop the heart of the Father. Pray through 1 John 3:16–20 for yourself.

Review your memory passages and begin learning the last one.

Day 2

GRIEF FOR THE BROKENHEARTED

(Kathy) One day my friend Allyson's son, Logan, was playing with some toys under the kitchen table where Allyson and her sister-in-law, Becky Baker, were having coffee. Aunt Becky is his favorite baby sitter: sweet, fun, and absolutely devoted to him and his brothers. But that day, the sadness in her voice caught his attention, and he sat Indian-style under the table, listening. Aunt Becky was talking about the man she'd been dating for many months, saying she was now getting mixed signals. Her hopes for a wonderful future were dying. Hearing hurt in his Aunt Becky's voice, Logan emerged from under the table. Putting his little hand on her arm he said:

Aunt Becky, he's just a "Love-Forgetter."

It is so easy, John tells us, to say the words but fail to follow through. Isn't it wonderful that we serve a God who is not a Love-Forgetter?

2. Review how you see grief for the brokenhearted in the story of the prodigal son (Luke 15:11–32). How can you tell that the father was deeply concerned for his son?

_____

_____

3. What model of grief for the brokenhearted is given in 1 John 3:16?

_____

4. How does Paul elaborate on this in Romans 5:6–8?

_____

_____

5. Sing "Amazing Grace" in your personal time with God and then reflect on the following question: How does the willingness of Jesus to die for your sins show grief for the broken-hearted?

_____

_____

6. What does John go on to tell us in 1 John 3:17–18?

_____

_____

Love is much more than warm, fuzzy feelings. John is exposing that error, for that may be a counterfeit love. True love results in sacrifice. John mentions giving of our material goods as one example.

7. Why is grief for the brokenhearted necessary in order to carry out the above commands?

_____

Too often, when we perceive that the cost is going to be higher than we want to pay, we close the door on our hearts, or, as the King James Version puts it, we "shutteth up our com-passions" (1 John 3:17b KJV). We don't care enough about the plight of the brokenhearted to pay a cost.

Esther is a beautiful example of mercy in action, and she has much to teach us about grief for the brokenhearted. Read Esther 7 and 8 as an overview.

8. What do you see Esther doing in the following passages? What principle do you see in each case? How could you apply this principle to your own life?

A. Esther 4:15–16

What she did: _____

Principle: _____

Application: _____

B. Esther 7:3–4

What she did: _____

Principle: _____

Application: _____

After Esther pleaded for her life and the lives of her people, Xerxes was angry, and he took action against Haman. But after he had done that, he seemed to forget about the edict against Esther's people. He was making good on only *half* of Esther's request—the part that mattered to him. His queen was safe. But as far as reversing the edict for the holocaust against the Jews, that was a bit messy. Edicts could not be reversed. Because this was complicated, Xerxes shuts up his compassions. He was a Love-Forgetter.

Esther, in sharp contrast, remembers and follows through. If she had been only trying to save her own life, she would not have gone back, but, constrained by love, she returned to plead with Xerxes. Like God the Father, she identifies with her people. She hears their cries of distress. Her heart breaks because their hearts are breaking. Dr. Joyce Baldwin writes:

> It is very moving to see the extent to which this young girl, who has everything money can buy, identifies herself with her own kith and kin, and is prepared to risk everything to prevent the disaster that threatens them.[4]

9. Describe Esther's emotion and words as she returns to Xerxes in Esther 8:3–6. How is Esther exemplifying the kind of true love John talks about?

_____

_____

_____

Each of us who has been delivered from hell can be *so* thankful for that deliverance. But how can the love of God be in us if we are satisfied with our portion and shut up our compassions to those who are still in the dark?

Consider John's phrase "shut up your compassions." It is a self-protective response. It takes faith to live in a way where your heart always remains open to those in need, believing God

will be with you. It takes even more faith when you do not see immediate results, but you must be like Esther and persist, for if you do not, how can the love of God be in you? John has mentioned giving of our material resources. It is also vital that we care enough about the lost to give of our spiritual resources.

(Kathy) My friend Ellie has truly done that in her neighborhood, but it wasn't easy for her. When she moved from New York to Virginia, she went through severe culture shock. She felt "normal" in New York, where demonstrative Italian women are everywhere, but in Rustin, Virginia, Ellie said, "I talked too fast, was too bold, and my hair was too big." In her book, *Slices of Life,*[5] Ellie tells her story. At first, she was very intimidated by the "blonde women."

> *They were not the blonde women from blonde women jokes. My blonde women were smart, sophisticated, articulate, talented, athletic, accessorized, and very thin . . . and those were just some of the reasons I did not like them. They just smiled and nodded and smiled and nodded. I could never tell what they were thinking.*

Yet the Lord impressed on her heart that she was to love her neighbor. Ellie argued:

> *You don't mean right next door—do you, God? Not the blonde women! I'll give to the homeless, I'll visit the prisoner, but do I really have to love the blonde woman? How can I even get to them, Lord? They drive up to their houses, click their garage door openers, and disappear as the door slides down behind them.*

God impressed on Ellie's heart that behind the smiles of some of the accessorized blonde women were unfulfilled hearts. He *was* calling her to be His love to them. When she prayed about how to gain credibility with them, she remembered something speaker Daisy Hepburn had told her: "Ellie, you cannot lead people until you first serve them."

"Serving the blonde women took surrender," Ellie said. "It was the beginning of real obedience." Ellie joined the PTA and volunteered at her children's school cafeteria, opening milk cartons and occasionally wiping up vomit. One day in the grocery store an excited little boy went running up to Ellie, recognizing her, tugging on her jacket.

"Mommy, Mommy," he cried to a sophisticated woman dressed in heels and an Ann Taylor suit. "It's the cafeteria lady!" Shaking her head, Ellie said:

> *It was so humbling for me. I wanted to say, "I had a radio show in New York! I have a master's degree in English! I used to be somebody!" But the Lord quieted me and reminded me of His love. I smiled and talked to her instead about what a great son she had.*

Ellie kept serving, kept praying, kept seeking ways to be His love to her neighbors. Finally, like a contemporary Esther, she took the plunge. She walked around her neighborhood, knocking on thirty-three doors, inviting each woman to Bible study. Three came, and Ellie felt *that* was a miracle. The first meeting was low-key and nonthreatening. They laughed through some fun get-acquainted questions, enjoyed good food, and listened attentively as a friend of Ellie's briefly shared how Bible study had changed her life. Ellie reflected:

> *We have something so wonderful to share—we just can't hide it and keep it under a bushel. In New York, when there was a great sale on tomatoes, the Italian women would call and tell each other. Why are we so hesitant to tell people about the secret that leads to eternal life? I told these women: You take care of yourselves physically—you'll go to a gym—you'll take care of yourselves intellectually—you read good books—but you must also take care of yourself spiritually!*

The study Ellie chose was a basic one to introduce them to Jesus. As the weeks passed, excitement began to bubble up—hearts were being softened, eyes opened, and one by one, the women began to place their trust in Christ. John tells us that "the whole world is under the control of the evil one" (1 John 5:19), but now those chains were falling off. The truth was setting them free, and their joy was contagious. More neighbors began to come. Ellie said:

> *Who is more fun than new Christians? A whole new world has opened up to them. I remember our first "field trip." They piled into a minivan and we headed to a large Baptist bookstore in Springfield, Virginia. They were astounded—their eye blink rate practically ceased as they walked about in Christian Wonderland: the children's section, the women's section, the music section. . . . These women had a lot of spending power. They all bought Bibles, and while their names were being engraved on the covers, they filled their arms with VeggieTales stuff, T-shirts, books, and tapes.*
>
> *I took the same group to Women of Faith. Same thing. Their jaws hung open as they looked around at 18,000 women singing praises to Jesus. Unless they were at a piano bar, they hadn't sung in years—and now they were singing their hearts out to Jesus!*

Ellie continues to have outreach coffees at Christmas, Valentine's Day, or to celebrate back-to-school for the kids. Today there are fifty-two women in that study, and their space and childcare needs have caused them to move the study to a nearby church.

10. What stood out to you in Ellie's story?

_____

11. Be still before the Lord, and ask Him to impress upon your heart the names or faces of people in your life who are brokenhearted. How might you be His love to them by sharing your material, spiritual, or emotional resources?

_____

_____

Day 3

FORGIVENESS FOR THE TRANSGRESSOR

Perhaps the most challenging way to be like the Father is in forgiveness. When we have been genuinely hurt, it is not natural to forgive. Forgive that mother-in-law, neighbor, or friend for what she said? Why, her words cut to the heart! No, the natural response is to want to make her pay. But if we are going to be "like Him in this world" (1 John 4:17b), we must forgive. We must let the offense go.

How can we possibly do this? Only by His Spirit, only by His grace. It is vital that we focus not on the offense but on how we have been forgiven, how the merciful Father washed us and made us as white as snow, remembering our sin no more.

It would be wonderful to sing this or pray it as you are alone with God:

> *What can wash away my sin?*
> *Nothing but the blood of Jesus.*
> *What can make me pure within?*
> *Nothing but the blood of Jesus.*
>
> *O precious is the flow*
> *That makes me white as snow.*
> *No other fount I know;*
> *Nothing but the blood of Jesus*
> (Public Domain)

Read Matthew 18:21–35.

12. What happened in the above parable? What is the primary lesson?

_____

_____

_____

13. Look again at the parable of the prodigal son in Luke 15:11–32. In what ways did the younger son hurt his father? List them. Then list the ways the older son hurt the father.

_____

_____

14. In what ways have you hurt the heart of the Father God?

_____

_____

In sign language, the motion for forgive is to take the fingertips of one hand and brush them across the open palm of the other hand in an outward direction, away from yourself, wiping the offense away. God has cleansed us, wiping the offense away, making us as white as snow. There is only one sin that God cannot forgive, and that is rejection of His Son, for we are rejecting our only lifeline. There is a difficult passage at the end of John's letter that seems to allude to this sin. It is in the context of prayer, when John is exhorting us to have mercy and to pray for our fallen brothers. John writes:

> _If anyone sees his brother commit a sin that does not lead to death, he should pray and God will give him life. I refer to those whose sin does not lead to death. There is a sin that leads to death. I am not saying that he should pray about that._ (1 John 5:16)

John Stott explains that all through his letter John has been differentiating between the real and the counterfeit. There are those who claim to be "brothers," who are, in fact, not brothers at all. In reality, they have rejected Christ.[6] With the exception of the sin of rejecting Christ, we can pray for any other sin to be forgiven.

15. Do you remember when you first came to Christ and He forgave you and cleansed you? If you remember anything about that time and how you felt, or how He changed your heart, share it briefly with the group.

_____

_____

16. What does Ephesians 4:32 tell us?

_____

_____

_____

Sing "Amazing Grace" in your personal quiet time, thanking the Lord for His mercy toward you.

17. Forgiveness is a gift we bestow on others who do not deserve it. It demands sacrifice on our part. How do we become like God when we give this gift?

_____

18. Sometimes people confuse forgiveness and trust. Do you see a difference? If so, what is it?

_____

_____

19. Is there someone to whom you need to give the gift of forgiveness? If so, who? How will you do it?

_____

_____

Continue learning your memory verse.

Day 4

GENEROSITY TOWARD THOSE IN NEED

We show the mercy of the Father through grief, forgiveness, and, finally, through generosity. We must love not only with words, but also with actions. James makes the same point John does, but with humor:

> *Suppose a brother or sister is without clothes and daily food. If one of you says to him, "Go, I wish you well; keep warm and well fed," but does nothing about his physical needs, what good is it?* (James 2:15–16)

There are some striking similarities between the letter of James and this letter of John's. Both are saying that, yes, we are saved by grace, but if there is no evidence of Jesus living in us, it makes no sense! God is exceedingly generous, so if He is truly living in us, we will do more than just wish our hurting brother well. We will give him or her our time, our love, our resources.

20. How did you see generosity in the father in the parable of the prodigal son?

_____

(Dee) Kathy has a friend who has undergone an amazing transformation into a beautiful bride. Claudette Rondanelli had been a drug addict, a topless dancer, and in her own words, "had a mouth like a truck driver and dressed like a prostitute." I believe that Kathy's response to Claudette shows us a model of generosity in action—a generosity of time, of spirit, and of love.

When I interviewed Claudette, she told me that when she had first met Kathy, she was not interested in talking to her.

"Why not?" I asked.

> *Kathy was a born-again Christian. I didn't like born-again people. Every one I met was a hypocrite and very mean. Not only that, she was famous. That was like two things against her. I just didn't want nothin' to do with her.*

Claudette's sister-in-law, Dorothy, was a friend of Kathy's. Dorothy played piano in a band at bars on Long Island. Claudette would often go to watch the band. Claudette said:

> *Kathy would come and see my sister-in-law play. I'd be drinking, a little toasted, and she'd come over and say, "How you doing, Claudette, so good to see you." She was always consistent. She was always loving.*

(Kathy) The first time I met Claudette I was a little intimidated by her. She had deep, dark eyes and long, thick, dark hair and a constant cigarette in her mouth. She definitely looked like a "rock-and-roll chick." But despite the fact that she didn't have a warmth or an openness in communication, God just gave me a heart for her. Whenever I would see her, I thought, *I just need to love this girl.* So often we demand people to make a change before we show them the love of Christ. We want the world to act like Christians before they even know Christ. (Acting like Christians is not necessarily a good thing—*acting like Jesus* is a good thing.) We want the alcoholic to lay down his drink long enough for us to pontificate about our beliefs. We want the single mother with three kids to immediately come to church on Sunday, even though she works fifty hours a week. We can imagine countless scenarios.

When I first decided to follow Jesus, He didn't say: "Now Kathy, before we start relationship here, just do me a favor. Stop being so angry. Stop abusing laxatives. Lose some weight. Don't fight with your mother so much." Can you imagine? And we can all come up with our own list of how God found us. Jesus doesn't require us to give up our gods and our addictions until we truly meet Him and know what we're giving them up for—that's when He wants us to get serious about it. We need to love people just as they are because that's how Jesus loved us.

(Dee) We are going to look at this secret in depth tomorrow, but I want you to see that what drew Claudette to Kathy was the love of Christ. John tells us:

> *No one has ever seen God; but if we love one another, God lives in us and his love is made complete in us.* (1 John 4:12)

Do you see? As we live in love, we make the invisible God visible. That's what Claudette was being drawn to:

> Kathy was always really warm and would ask me about my life, about my kid. I wasn't that eager to talk to her, and I was a little standoffish, but she'd sit down and just keep asking me about myself.
>
> One night I went to her house with Dorothy. Dorothy cooked and Kathy just talked to me. My back hurt and she came around my chair and gently rubbed my shoulders. After a while I started asking her a few questions. She was able to express her heart without condemnation—and she didn't talk to me about any of my "stuff." She just talked to me about Jesus. She talked about Him like He was her husband. He was so real to her. She was so in love with Him. I thought . . . I want that.
>
> What I loved about Kathy was that she was human. There are a lot of Christians who walk around and pretend that they come to Jesus and everything's fine. But I'd see Kathy cry, or get bummed out. She was normal. Some Christians put on a front and you think, Something's wrong here. Kathy was real, but Jesus' love was in her. That's what drew me. I was starting to open up, asking her anything I wanted.
>
> One day she said, "Claudette, it sounds like you want to know more. Why don't you come to church with me?"
>
> I said, "Yeah, yeah, okay." I didn't, though, and when she'd see me, she'd mention it again. Finally I promised.
>
> That next Saturday night I went out with my boss and got very high because we went to a wedding. I woke up with a hangover, but I thought, You know, I made a promise. So I went with Kathy and Dorothy.
>
> I saw everyone singing and praying. I told them, "I'm not going to sing, I'm not going to do anything. I'm just going to sit here."
>
> They said, "You can do whatever you want."
>
> So I sat there and started getting touched by the Holy Spirit. I didn't know that at the time. I was just reading the words of the songs off the screen. There was such a lump in my throat, like a watermelon. I was gasping for air. I leaned over and said, "What's going on here? I feel like I'm going to choke."
>
> But immediately they responded: "Oh, that's the Holy Spirit."
>
> The next week I went back with them. When we were walking into church we were talking about some stuff from the Bible. It nearly knocked me over when the pastor's sermon was on the same stuff. Afterward, I told him about that and he said, "Isn't God good?"
>
> I said, "Well . . . yeah . . ."
>
> Then he asked me if I had received Jesus as my personal Savior and Lord. I told him no.
>
> He said, "Why not?"
>
> I said, "I'm afraid."
>
> But that was the day I did.

"Love drives out fear" (1 John 4:18). The transformation was beginning in Claudette.

The next day I was running around trying to find a Bible. I'm like, "I can't find a Bible. Are there places around to get Bibles?" So Kathy bought me The Living Bible. *I started reading and God started working in my life very quickly.*

Though Claudette did not know the principles in 1 John, the Holy Spirit was leading her in them. He was drawing her to the light and drawing her to die to her old way of life:

Some of my stuff went away right away—like my foul mouth. I changed the way I dressed. My husband said, "Where's the sexy woman I married?"
I said, "She's become a lady."
Other stuff took a long time—like my smoking. For thirty years I'd had a pack a day. I couldn't seem to stop. But two years ago I asked God to make me hate it, and I got a terrible upper respiratory infection. That did it.

As Claudette was dying to the old, there was room for the new. Like crocuses that push through the snow, Claudette's spirit was coming to life. She developed a real love for the Bible, and as she poured truth into her soul, the flowers were spreading in wondrous profusion. The fourth principle, that of showing mercy, began to take hold in her life—something that amazed her.

I really want to be a praying and loving mother and grandmother. One of the biggest things was that I really didn't like people before—and I didn't have time for kids. But now I work in a special education school. So many in my family have come to Christ. My mom is just sixteen years older than me, and now she loves Jesus too. I work in a ministry for Long Island Citizens for Community Values. It's a ministry to help people who have been sexually violated.

(Kathy) Claudette has a great big heart and has blessed me so much. Last year I asked her to come to my New Year's Party. It's my big party every year, and it's become a tradition that my guests participate in a talent show. Some of the "acts" are funny, and some of them are serious. Claudette had been learning sign language and had learned to do it with my song "Lord, I Need You Now" from my very first recording, *Stubborn Love*. So I asked her if she would do it that night for my party. I watched in awe as Claudette tenderly expressed a prayer I sang way back in 1982 before my guests. I just started to cry because I thought, *Dear God, You do make beauty out of ashes.*

21. What can you learn from Kathy's model in loving Claudette?

_____

_____

22. What can you learn from Jesus' model of generosity?

_____

_____

23. Each of us needs to give of our material resources on a regular basis. How do you decide to whom to give?

_____

_____

There are *so* many needs in the world, it would be easy to be overwhelmed to the point that you end up doing *nothing*. But each of us is called to do *something*. It is important to support your local church and to be open to supporting other ministries. (If you don't know where to start, we have listed a few Web sites of ministries in the Resources at the back of the book. Dee and her husband, Steve, know individuals in each of these ministries whom they trust and who have testified to how the money is being used. These ministries all belong to the Evangelical Counsel for Financial Accountability.)

Don't give rashly, but instead be prayerful and seek the Lord about your giving. Not every ministry that claims to be Christian is, in fact, Christian. Counterfeits abound. But there are wonderful ministries that reflect the heart of God.

It is also vital to be sensitive to the leading of the Holy Spirit. God brings people into our lives and puts them on our minds on a regular basis. We must remain sensitive, or we will miss seeing the people God is bringing directly to us. It is to these people that we must be generous, seeking ways to be His love to them.

Our human tendency is to shut up our hearts, so pray about doing God's will in your heart, using the following Scriptures:

> 1 John 3:16–17
> Isaiah 58:6–9
> 2 Corinthians 9:6–15

Day 5

MAY I BE HIS LOVE TO YOU

Do you remember John's amazing promise in the prologue? He said that just as he saw Jesus with his own eyes, and touched Him, so can we! We can have that same intimacy with Him.

How exciting to come to this part in John's letter and to have this mystery unveiled. Do you know *how* we can see Him and hear Him and touch Him? It is through one another!

As we truly love one another, showing mercy not just in word but in actions, we manifest Jesus to one another. This is one way we can tangibly love Jesus and be loved by Him. Yes, Jesus will be intimate with us on a one-to-one basis, but He is also intimate with us through the different individuals who make up His Bride. We are absolutely breathtaking to Him—we are embroidered with gold when we are His love to one another.

(Dee) There were times in my life when John's letters seemed a bit like a broken record to me. Over and over he seemed to keep saying, "Love one another." Here again, in chapter 4, the words seemed to repeat. So I read it quickly, thinking, *Okay, okay—I know this!* But then one day I slowed down, making observations, the way I know I should. Suddenly what seemed so simple was incredibly profound. The mystery revealed.

In 1 John 4:7–17, John is actually showing us the secret to the promise he made in his prologue, when he told us that we could have the same intimacy with Jesus as he and the other disciples had. Read it carefully to discover its profound truths.

24. Meditate on 1 John 4:7–17.

    A. (v.7) The one who *truly* loves (not just warm, fuzzy feelings) is demonstrating something. What is it and why?

    _____

    _____

    B. (v. 8) What is the corollary to the above truth?

    _____

    C. (vv. 9–10) How did Christ live this kind of love? How did His sacrifice demonstrate all three aspects of mercy (grief for the brokenhearted, forgiveness for the sinner, and generosity)?

    _____

    _____

    _____

    _____

    D. (vv. 11–13) What is the exhortation, and then, what are the promises?

    _____

    _____

    _____

    E. Read carefully this comment from *The Bible Knowledge Commentary:*

    The indwelling God, whose presence is manifested in the midst of a loving Christian community, thus becomes in a sense truly visible to the eye of faith. Though no one "has seen" (tetheatai, "beheld") God (v. 12), believers who abide in Him (v. 13) "have seen" (tetheameta, "behold") the Son as He is manifested among loving Christians. . . . With these words, John reached the goal he had announced in the prologue (1:1–4), namely, that his readers might share the apostles' experience. The term "life" in 1:2, though it refers to Christ incarnate, nevertheless was carefully chosen by the writer. What his readers could witness is the renewed manifestation of that life in their fellow Christians. But, as he had argued ever since 2:29, the "life" which Christians possess by new birth is inherently sinless and can only be manifested through righteousness and Christlike love. But when that occurs, Christ whom the apostles saw in the flesh is, in a real but spiritual sense, "seen" again.[7]

John goes on in 4:14–17 to review that those who sincerely believe the truth (that Jesus is the Savior, the Son of God) can manifest Him to one another. God lives in them! As we manifest Him to one another, we give one another a *fresh* experience of faith.

Has the genuine love of other believers, as seen in their forgiveness, or generosity, or compassion, given you a fresh experience of faith? Has it enabled you to see Jesus, hear Jesus, touch Jesus? If so, share a specific example.

_____

_____

F. Can you think of a time in your life when the Lord allowed you to be the love of Jesus to someone else, so that, through you, they could actually see Jesus, hear Jesus, or touch Jesus? If so, when? What do you remember?

_____

_____

G. Meditate on 1 John 4:15–16. What is it saying?

_____

_____

25. What do you think you will remember about this week's lesson? Why?

_____

_____

Review your memory passage.

If you would like, pray the following chorus for yourself in your personal quiet time.

"MAY I BE HIS LOVE"

> *May I be His love for you*
> *May I lift your eyes toward heaven*

May I come to you and lead you to His light
May I cry His tears for you
May I be the place that you can run to
Where you'll hear His voice
And see Him in my eyes
All your life may I be His love

PRAYER TIME

Begin with a time of praise, thinking of specific ways God has been, to you, like the father in the story of the prodigal son. Then lift up a specific prayer request for yourself and allow a few other women to support you with sentence prayers.

You may wish to close with the above theme song or this one:

In my life, Lord, be glorified, be glorified
In my life, Lord, be glorified today.
In Your Bride, Lord, be glorified, be glorified
In Your Bride, Lord, be glorified today.

Week 10: CLOTHED IN THE MANY-SPLENDORED COLORS OF HIS LOVE

"The royal daughter is all glorious within the palace; her clothing is woven with gold. She shall be brought to the King in robes of many colors."
(PSALM 45:13–14A NKJV)

CLOTHED IN THE MANY-SPLENDORED COLORS OF HIS LOVE

This week, there will be no video in order to give you more time for the valuable review. It is possible your group will decide to divide this review into two weeks. This is the most important lesson for the following reasons:

- You have looked at pieces of the puzzle. This week, you will look at the whole picture.
- The Spirit can help you to crystallize what you have spent months discovering.
- Questions for reflection will encourage you in application, which is where the transformation takes place. Find a quiet place to meet with God, and ask Him to help you be still and to hear.

Day 1

WHAT IS SHE WEARING?

Review your memory passages from Weeks 1–3.

When we're really honest with ourselves, we have to admit there are often times when we certainly are not clothed in the colors of His love. So often we fail to love; we fail to care about those around us:

> The weary waitress
> The coworker grieving the loss of a marriage
> The believer who has failed dramatically
> The "trying" relative that you see every Christmas

Often our lives lack the passion and vibrancy of a life surrendered to God. We want to be women who love well, but our cups do not overflow with God's love. We want to walk in the light, but we find ourselves moving into the shadows. Like Tinkerbell in *Peter Pan* when she was losing her power, our lights are dim and our colors are faded. We become dull, like an empty midnight sky. We are no longer stars that glitter in a dark universe. We lack beauty, luster, and life.

As in the story Jesus told of the good Samaritan, we step over the needy or wounded, preoccupied with our own agenda.

"THE GOOD SAMARITAN"
JACOPO BASSANO (1517/18–1592)

1. When Jesus told the story of the good Samaritan, He was not saying, necessarily, that the Samaritan was a believer. What *was* He saying? (Week 2)

_____

_____

2. The Pharisees were making the mark of a Christian something quite different from what Jesus said was most important. What were the Pharisees emphasizing? How can we fall into the same trap?

_____

_____

John gives tests for doctrinal truth in his letter, but Jesus also makes it clear that this is not how the *world* will measure a Christian's authenticity. At the Last Supper, after Jesus had washed their feet, He gave His disciples a new command.

"CHRIST WASHING PETER'S FEET"
FORD MADOX BROWN (1821–1893)

3. Read John 13:33–35.

    A. Why was the timing of this "new command" significant?

    _____

    B. What was the new command?

    _____

    C. What effect would obedience to this command have on people in the world?

    _____

    _____

4. Review Jesus' prayer for us in John 17:20–23.

    A. When did He pray this, and why is the timing significant?

    _____

    B. What did He pray?

    _____

    C. Why did He pray this?

    _____

In your personal quiet time, sing:

> *Beloved, let us love one another*
> *For love is of God*
> *And everyone who loveth is born of God*
> *And knoweth God*
> *He who loveth not*
> *Knoweth not God*
> *For God is love*
> *Beloved, let us love one another*
> *First John, four, seven and eight*

5. Often we fail to love well because we are trying to love in our own strength. As you reflect on the prevailing theme of 1 John, as seen in the above verse, what is different about this approach? Have you seen any growth in your love toward other believers in

the last few months? What evidence have you seen in attitudes or actions? (Don't share this in the group. It can simply be a personal encouragement if you are seeing more of the love of Jesus flow from you to others.)

_____

_____

_____

6. If you rub a crayon over a paper covering a leaf, you can see its shape, its veins, its stem. The identity of the tree that gave it birth becomes evident. In the same way, we should reflect the One who gave us birth. Find some "black-and-white" statements from 1 John that indicate either our Father is God, or our father is Satan.

_____

_____

_____

_____

The life of a man who professes to be living
in God must bear the stamp of Christ. (1 John 2:6 PHILLIPS)

The above statements can make us want to run for the hills, for we realize how short we fall. It is in our very nature to size people up by the way they look, by the way they dress, by the way they talk, and even by how much money they have.

We are easily offended. And when we are genuinely wronged, we often have trouble letting it go. Unwilling to forgive, unwilling to let our wounds heal, we peer over a wall of compiled offenses, holding our weapons of anger and self-righteousness.

Our thought lives reveal our hearts—and so often, our thoughts are impure and unkind. We may be thinking unlovely things about a person, yet a stream of lovely words pours out of our mouths. We cover the truth of what we are feeling with "Christian niceties," but the judgment and bitterness of our hearts condemn us.

We are preoccupied with thoughts about how we look, what others are thinking about us, what we're planning to eat, or watch, or do. . . . It's all about us.

Let's face it. The old hymn writers dared to call us "wretches" or even "worms"—and though those terms may be politically incorrect, when we get real, we have to confess that they hit the mark. In the midst of a philosophical discussion, a young woman reminded Winston Churchill: "We are all worms."

Churchill turned to the young woman and said, "Perhaps, Violet—but I am a glowworm."[1]

The truth is, we are more flawed and lost than we ever dared believe. Yet we also, if we are trusting in Christ, have One living in us that is more glorious and powerful than we ever dared hope. We are wretched women, but we can be transformed into beautiful brides through the mighty power of God living in us.

7. The Scriptures speak of a bride adorned in white. Do you remember what the wedding garment represents? (Week 1)

_____

_____

"THE FOOLISH VIRGINS"
JAMES TISSOT (1836–1902)

The evidence is strong that the five virgins who were not prepared were counterfeit believers. Unless you have the Spirit of God living in you, you cannot love well nor are you ready for your Bridegroom's return. Your own strength, like the oil in the unprepared virgins' lamps, will run out.

8. Review John's teaching in 1 John 3:2–3. What does he say? How does this relate to the parable of the ten virgins?

_____

_____

9. The four principles we have studied in 1 John are all characteristics of God. List each principle and show how it is true of God, giving a Scripture reference from 1 John to support your statement.

Light: _____

Death:_____

Truth: _____

Mercy:_____

Because these characteristics are true of the Lord, abiding in Him, surrendering to Him, and allowing Him to flow through you are the secrets to being transformed. Don't try to do it in your own strength! The mighty power of God lives in you.

10. Of the above four principles, which has had the greatest impact on you and why?

_____

_____

_____

Pray through Psalm 45:10–14 for yourself.

Day 2

CLOTHED IN LIGHT

Review your memory passages from Weeks 4–5.

Read the first two chapters of 1 John as a review.

(Dee) When Kathy and I were at the event where they had the lovely bridal theme to bless women in ministry, we felt strongly led to anoint the women with oil. I had never done this, and at first was hesitant. Could I do this, according to the Word? (Remember that one of the characteristics of truth is that it does not conflict with God's Word.)

As I studied anointing in the Old Testament, I saw that it was done for kings and for priests, as indicative of God's presence, of the Spirit of God. Suddenly, I realized: Under the new covenant, *every* believer is a priest! (1 Peter 2:9). These women in ministry could be blessed by a literal anointing that would represent the anointing of the Holy Spirit.

As we anointed these women we found ourselves whispering: "You are His Bride" or "You are His Beloved." It was such a sweet reminder of what John told believers in his letter. In 1 John 2:12–14, he pauses and addresses believers in various levels of maturity—from those who have just come into relationship with God to those who have known the Lord for a long time. John's words were running through my mind as I allowed the Spirit to bless these women in ministry. As I anointed them, I reminded them of the mighty promises of God:

> *Dear child, your sins have been forgiven.*
> *Dear woman, you know Him who has been from the beginning.*
> *Young girl, you have overcome the evil one because the Word of God lives in you.*
> (Based on 1 John 2:12–14)

The oil was simply a symbol of the Spirit. Every believer, though she may not be *literally* anointed with oil, absolutely *must* be anointed by the Spirit, or her ministry will be of no avail. We *must* allow God's light, death, truth, and mercy to live through us. Then the oil will run down, flowing into the lives of those around us. Charles Spurgeon reminds us that we must go daily to the Holy Ghost that we may have our heads anointed with oil. How do we do that? We ask, in prayer, for His Spirit to be with us through the day. Then we walk, throughout the day, in continual and genuine repentance.

Aaron was anointed as a priest, yet he completely quenched the Spirit by allowing the impatient people to build and worship a gold calf. Likewise, King Saul was anointed, but he walked in the ways of man and quenched the Spirit. It is significant that the final act in his life was to visit the witch of Endor. King David was anointed with oil, but in contrast, he walked in genuine repentance. What an enormous difference, and what a lesson for us.

God tells us these true stories to teach us. He teaches us, as well, through the story of Cain. When we move out of the light and into the shadows, God's Spirit convicts us. If we do not learn how to respond to the Spirit of God when He convicts us through His Word, through a "holy twist" in our gut, or through the pain of our sorry circumstances, we become like Cain.

Cain's name has become synonymous with darkness. He is the antithesis of the imprint of Christ—instead of reflecting Christ, he reflects the face of the evil one who was given free reign in his heart. He was a liar and a murderer. Cain was not a believer, for John says he belonged to the evil one. But don't assume that because you are a believer, you are immune from being overpowered by sin. John's letter was written to believers, and he warns believers: "Do not be like Cain" (1 John 3:12a).

"CAIN SLAYING ABEL"
PETER PAUL RUBENS (1577–1640)

11. Review Genesis 4:1–10 and list the three opportunities that Cain was given to do the right thing. What did he choose each time, and what were the consequences?

_____

_____

_____

12. Review everything John's letter teaches about Cain in 1 John 3:10–15.

_____

_____

_____

13. What are some reasons God longs for you to turn from the darkness and choose the light? How can you specifically apply the lessons learned from Cain to your life?

_____

_____

_____

14. Review what John teaches about walking in the light in 1 John 1:5–10.

_____

_____

_____

15. Review what John teaches about walking in the light in 1 John 2:7–11.

_____

_____

_____

16. Living in continual repentance is the key to walking in the light. Define true repentance and then give an example, either from Scripture or your own life.

_____

_____

Many of us, particularly as women, like to _feel_ things and hold on to them. Somehow it makes us feel more alive. Of course, emotion in itself is not bad, it's just that we can "camp around feelings" that cause destruction. We can settle into self-pity, anger, guilt, and all sorts of webs. That's why, especially as women, we may weep before God but do nothing about our self-made prisons. They have become comfortable to us. Gut-wrenching emotion is one kind of counterfeit repentance.

17. Review how the men in Malachi 2 exemplified "gut-wrenching" emotion without a U-turn.

_____

_____

18. We studied two other forms of counterfeit repentance. Define them and then give an example of each from the life of King Saul.

Counterfeit # 2 _____

_____

Counterfeit # 3 _____

_____

19. What kind of counterfeit repentance are you most likely to practice? Has this lesson impacted you? If so, how?

_____

_____

20. What are some ways God convicts you? Do you view conviction from the Holy Spirit as a gift? Why or why not?

_____

_____

21. What are some of the resources you have to help you stay in the light and live a holy life according to 1 John 2:12–14?

_____

_____

Pray through 1 John 1:5–9 for yourself. Then pray through 1 John 2:12–14 for yourself. In all of the above, note how the power is of God, and not of yourself.

Day 3

CLOTHED IN DEATH

Review your memory passages from Weeks 6–7.
 Read the third chapter of 1 John as a review.
 Prepare your heart by singing:

> *Seek ye first the Kingdom of God*
> *and His righteousness,*
> *and all these things will be added unto you*
> *Allelu, Alleluia.*

(*Kathy*) One October morning I made some coffee and sat down at the kitchen table facing a huge bay window, marveling at the breathtaking autumn scene. The most gifted painter couldn't possibly capture what God displayed that morning before my eyes. All these brilliant colors of fall made the yard look so alive, yet I was reminded that there was a process of dying going on. In the midst of the splendor, each leaf would soon fall, decay, and turn the color of death. In a month the trees would be bare, the ground barren. It would be hard to imagine the backyard vibrant with color again, but new life would emerge in the spring.

It's the same way with us. I had to laugh when Dee told me about a cartoon of Katherine Kuhlman praying over an overweight person and saying, "Be healed of obesity." How I wished that were the case in 1978. I would have loved it if, after I invited Jesus into my heart, I had awakened a new creation at my ideal weight. Instead it took work, it took discipline, it took dying to myself. But today I am in a place of rejoicing.

22. Is there an area in your life where you have trusted God enough to die and you have seen Him create new life? If so, share something about it.

_____

_____

23. Review 1 John 2:15–17. Define each of these three false values.

_____

_____

_____

24. According to John in v. 17, why should we die to the above false values?

_____

_____

25. Consider each of these areas prayerfully before God, asking Him where you could trust Him enough to die so that new life could come. (You don't need to share this in the group.)

A. The lust of the flesh_____

_____

B. The lust of the eyes_____

_____

C. The pride of life _____

_____

26. As you consider the story of Esther, how did pride often cause problems in relationships?

_____

_____

27. In your own life, are there relationships that could be closer if you would trust God enough to die to your pride? How honest are you with the people in your life? How willing are you to admit when you are wrong, to take a servant role, to be vulnerable? Pride hides the colors of His love, like the overbearing chlorophyll in the leaves.

Be still and allow God's light to shine in your heart. What relationships could be closer if you died to pride? Ask God to be specific with you concerning how to die.

_____

_____

28. We are more flawed and lost than we think. Yet we belong to a God who is a Redeemer, who can bring beauty out of ashes. How did you see this in the book of Esther?

_____

_____

29. To what did Mordecai need to die? To what did Esther need to die? What happened as a result of their willingness to die?

_____

_____

30. How did Esther exemplify real love, as defined in 1 John 3:16?

_____

FRESCO OF ESTHER
ANDREA DEL CASTAGNO
(1423–1457)

31. What will you remember about Esther as an encouragement? Be specific.

_____

_____

CLOTHED IN TRUTH

Review your memory passage from Week 8.
    Read the fourth chapter of 1 John as a review.

You might prepare your heart by singing:

> *Greater is He that is in me*
> *Greater is He that is in me*
> *Greater is He that is in me*
> *Than he that is in the world*

Words and Music by Lanny Wolfe ©1973 Lanny Wolfe Music Co. All Rights Reserved. Used by Permission.

John explains that the Antichrist, the one who will war against Christ, is coming. *Before* he comes, his way is being prepared by "many antichrists," or, as theologian John Stott explains, "a spirit of antichrist at work in the world."[2] This spirit is as old as our ancient foe and truly *reigns* in our world today. It's in our movies, our talk shows, our universities, our women's magazines, and in the minds and mouths of those who do not know God.

32. Review the following signs for the counterfeit:

    A. The ultimate lie (1 John 2:22) _____

    _____

    B. 1 John 2:19 _____

    _____

    C. 1 John 4:5–6 _____

    _____

33. What are our sources of truth (1 John 2:14 and 2:20), and why should they agree?

    _____

    _____

34. The people to whom we are closest have a huge impact on our lives. According to the
    following passages, describe the impact people had on one another in the book of Esther.

    A. Esther 1:13–21 _____

B. Esther 2:2–4 _____

_____

C. Esther 3:8–15 _____

_____

35. How do the above incidents demonstrate the truth of 1 John 4:1–5?

_____

_____

36. The spirit of antichrist tolerates all people except one. How do you see this in Esther 3:8?

_____

37. Review Mordecai's famous speech to Esther in Esther 4:13–14 in which he speaks the truth to her. What three reasons does he use to persuade her to go to Xerxes? What does each mean?

_____

_____

_____

38. How is Esther impacted?

_____

_____

39. Think about those who are closest to you and how they impact you spiritually. Be still before the Lord, asking Him if you need to seek out stronger friends. Also, ask Him what kind of impact you are having on those closest to you.

_____

_____

Day 5

CLOTHED IN MERCY

Review your memory passage from Week 9.

Read the fifth chapter of 1 John as a review.

(Dee) An adventure in my life involved Hari, a dynamic young man from Nepal. Hari had put his trust in Christ before we met him, but his nineteen-year-old bride had not. Rita was

terribly homesick—missing her mother and father, language, warm climate, and Nepalese food. One day our pastor came to the house with Hari, asking if I would consider having Hari and Rita move in with us, at least until Rita adjusted to America and learned English. "She needs a mother here," our pastor said, his eyes pleading with me. "And our brother here," he said, nodding to Hari, "needs some help." Our pastor knew that Steve and I had been blessed with a large home, and that our two oldest children had moved out, leaving the downstairs, with a bed and bath, vacant. This verse came to me:

> *If anyone has material possessions and sees his brother in need*
> *but has no pity on him, how can the love of God be in him?* (1 John 3:17)

I struggled, as I often have in the past, with my own agenda. But I also was learning to trust the heart of Jesus, and to be open to His Spirit. I agreed to pray and let them know. I asked God to open my heart if this was His calling for me or to release me if it was not.

My heart began to turn toward this couple, and toward Rita, who was only a few years older than our own daughter, Sally. *How would I feel*, I thought, *if Sally were in a faraway land and homesick. Wouldn't I want a woman who loves Jesus to take her under her wing?*

Hari and Rita moved in. Rita immediately called me "Auntie," and Sally, "Sister." One of Hari's first requests was of Sally. He wanted her to help Rita shave her legs, which had never seen the blade of a razor. "Make her smooth," he asked, "like American women." Sally led a wide-eyed Rita into the bathroom, armed with shaving cream and a pink Lady Gillette. For more than an hour we heard shrieks and laughter over the sound of running water. When they emerged, Sally was drenched in perspiration and Rita was wreathed in smiles. She placed first one leg and then the other on a chair, taking my hand and running it over her smooth skin. It was a sweet moment as she smiled from ear to ear.

Another time we took Rita to our cabin in Wisconsin, where she was going to try swimming for the first time. We gave her a suit and she disappeared into the bedroom. When she came out, she had it on backward, with her breasts exposed, hanging freely. My girls clapped their hands over their mouths in astonishment. When Rita understood her mistake, we all collapsed on the floor in laughter.

Because Rita was just learning English, we used Bible picture books for children for our devotional times, trying to introduce her to Jesus. We acted out stories, just as we had done when our children were small, of Jesus calming the storm and healing the lepers. But somehow, the veil seemed to remain over Rita's eyes. She saw Jesus as an American God and planned to worship Buddha when she and Hari returned to Nepal. I have to admit I was discouraged. Yet I also knew I had responded with an open heart toward Rita. As always, the Holy Spirit would do the rest.

Eventually Hari and Rita moved into their own apartment and began their family. When Rita was pregnant with their second child, she became very ill. I'll never forget the phone call from the doctor telling us that further tests revealed that Rita was dying of cancer. Would Steve and I break the news to them?

Though we prayed desperately for healing, it was not to be. My last visit to Rita will live forever in my memory. Rita was on the couch, wrapped in blankets, pale and weak, holding their newborn son. Her face lit up when I came through the door. "Auntie!"

I told her not to talk, that I would just sit there with her, but Rita had something she had to tell me. She said, "Auntie, because of this . . . I see who Jesus is now." She told me how He had brought her His peace in the midst of her storm. Together, despite the tremendous sorrow, we wept tears of joy. I told Rita that I was praying she would not die. She had always seemed so childlike to me, but at that very moment, she became like a woman who had known Jesus for years, glimpsing a vision into the heavenlies:

"Auntie, Jesus is calling me home. He has shown me His glory. But Auntie, I need your help."

"Anything, Rita."

"Hari and I need you to find him a wife and a mother who will really love Angela and Andrew and teach them all about Jesus. Will you?"

I hesitated. Could I say a definite yes to this? But how could I not? Suddenly I was sobbing and promising.

Hari took Rita home to be with her parents in her final days. After her death he called me from Nepal, saying simply, "I desperately *need* a wife and a mother for my children." I told him I was praying and then we prayed together on the phone.

A few months later I was leading a Bible study. I remember the moment when Hari and his children came into my mind as I encountered Christy in the group. I had been impressed with her deep love for the Lord. But the lightbulb moment came when she told me: "I am *so* excited about my plans for spring break." I thought she was going to tell me about a mission trip, or a ski trip, but instead she said, "I'm going to take care of my friend's children while they go away for a week. I'm counting the days."

I remember asking the Lord, *Could she be the one?*

When I told Hari about Christy, he asked me to set up ten dates with her. I had to hold back my laughter. I said, "Hari, that's not how we do it in America. If Christy agrees, I'll set you up for the first date, and we'll pray that if God is in it, that she will agree to see you again."

God had gone before Hari and Christy. They fell deeply in love, but even though they were older, and the need was great, they didn't rush. The children bonded with Christy, and it gave me joy to see them run into her arms whenever they saw her.

A year later Hari and Christy were married at a beautiful ceremony, where Angela was the flower girl, and Andrew the ring bearer. Today I absolutely marvel at what God has done. Because the children had been through so much trauma, they were out-of-control toddlers. But today they are happy and well behaved. They know God's Word, and they love not only one another, but their new baby sister as well. Christy is the wife and mother for whom Rita and I prayed, for our God is a God who answers prayer.

I had *no* idea when I invited Hari and Rita to live with us what the future held, but God did. All He asks of us is to be available and to keep our hearts open. If we ask Him to break our hearts with the things that break *His* heart, we *will* become actively involved in showing compassion.

You might prepare your heart by singing:

This is my commandment that you love one another
That your joy may be full
This is my commandment that you love one another
That your joy may be full

That your joy may be full
That your joy may be full

This is my commandment that you love one another
That your joy may be full.

One portrait the Lord gives us of mercy is that of the forgiving father.

"The Return of the Prodigal Son"
Rembrandt (1606–1669)

40. What three aspects of mercy do you see in the father in the above parable? (Week 9)
How do you see these aspects, or the lack of them, in yourself?

_____

_____

41. Did you see any of these aspects of mercy in the life of Esther? If so, how?

_____

_____

42. Review 1 John 3:18–22. Find all the promises for a transforming work of God occurring in you as you, by faith, love your brother and keep God's commandments.

_____

_____

43. What is John saying in 1 John 4:12–17? How is this a fulfillment of the promise made in the prologue (1 John 1:1–3)?

_____

_____

44. List some of the "takeaways" from this study. What will you still remember, perhaps a year from now, that can continue to transform you into a beautiful bride?

_____

_____

_____

_____

PRAYER TIME

Have a time of thanksgiving for the truths He has shown you in this study.

Pray for one another, that God will continue His transforming work. Be specific in praying about walking in the light, dying to oneself, discerning and embracing the truth, and showing mercy.

You might want to close by singing this chorus:

> _In my life, Lord, be glorified, be glorified_
> _In my life, Lord, be glorified today._
>
> _In your Bride, Lord, be glorified, be glorified_
> _In your Bride, Lord, be glorified today._

APPENDIX A: LEADER'S HELPS

FIRST THINGS:

Thank you for stepping out in faith to lead this study. We've prayed for you!

If you are hoping to interest women in coming to this study, we suggest showing the short promotional video:

- at your church.
- at a friend's home during a coffee in which you have invited friends (also have a woman prepared to give a short testimony on what Bible study has meant to her).
- at your retreat, Bible study, or kickoff for women's ministries.

If at all possible, have the women do their homework before the first week. If not, you will need to do the lesson together. Watch the video first, and then put the chairs in as small a circle as possible to facilitate sharing.

YOUR ROLE:

You are both a shepherd and a facilitator.

A SHEPHERD

Studies show the main reason women drop out of a study is because they do not feel cared for. Some ways to show love:

- At every meeting, warmly greet every woman who comes in the door.
- Affirm every answer with a nod, a smile, or even an encouraging comment. (If an answer is "off the wall," you can always say, "That's interesting!")
- Affirm group members whenever you can between meetings through e-mails, notes, calls—especially if someone has been absent. Let her know she was missed.
- Pray for each woman during the week, by name.
- Encourage caring between members by assigning prayer partners or secret sisters.
- Plan a fun movie night. We recommend that you look into finding Trimark's *Esther* video right away. You will begin studying Esther in Week 7, so a video night before then would be great. If your local Christian bookstore does not have it for rent, it can be purchased through Christianbook.com or Dee's ministry at deebrestin.com.

A DISCUSSION FACILITATOR

Your role is not to be a teacher, for the teacher is the Holy Spirit, but you can unleash His power through:

- Prayer.
- Sensitivity to facial expressions so you can draw shyer members out ("Kay, did you have a thought to add?").
- Keeping the ball bouncing from one group member to another rather than from you to a group member and back. Going around with questions occasionally can be good, but always give women the freedom to pass. If there is a wrong answer, you can pause and see if someone in the group gives a more accurate answer. If not, and you feel the error should not stand, then gently say, "Well, let's look at that passage again."
- Pacing yourself and your group. You may find your group does not have time to answer all the questions. If so, highlight the questions you want to be sure are answered, and pace the discussion. We've given suggestions in each week for questions we would highlight ahead of time so you can move more quickly. Don't discuss the video questions—move right to the "Icebreaker." Be sure to save time for the important question at the close of each study. If your group is large or you have less than two hours, you may need to divide the study by watching the video and doing two days the first week, and by doing the last three days and the prayer time the second week.

Common Problems to Anticipate

Women Not Doing Homework
- Some women feel that if there is a video, they don't need to do their homework. That is absolutely not true. It goes against everything that we are teaching in *Living in Love with Jesus*. The videos are meant to augment, rather than substitute for, their time alone with God.
- If you have a lethargic group, call a few of the more mature women and ask them to set an example for the others by doing their homework.
- Sometimes it's helpful to pair a more mature woman with a less mature woman and ask them to pray for each other and to keep one another accountable on their homework and memory work.
- Ask the Lord to show you when to give grace and when to admonish.

Monopolizers
- Often these women have special hurts, and it is important to pray for them, to minister to them outside the group, and to listen to them then.
- Try to sit next to rather than across from the monopolizer, for eye contact encourages her to share.
- Go around occasionally with questions or a statement such as: "Could we hear from someone who hasn't spoken yet?" (Then be alert to facial expressions—"Do you have a thought, Mary?")
- If the problem threatens to kill your group, you may need to gently go to the monopolizer, outside the group, and diplomatically explain that some are not having the chance to share, and that you need her *help* in drawing them out. A few ideas for what to say:

"You and I both love to talk, but we each need to hold back to help the shyer members have the time to find courage to share."

"I have appreciated many of the things you have said. My concern is for those who are not as free to share. Could you mark a couple of the answers you really want to give and hold back on the others so that we can give them silences to gather courage to share?"

OVERBURDENED

If you have a woman in your group going through a crisis, it is important to minister to her without swallowing up all the group time. Ideas:

- Find women in the group who can minister to her outside the group. It is our responsibility to help carry the burdens of those carrying heavy loads.

  This study is about loving one another—that is the most tangible way we can love Jesus, and this is an opportunity for your group to put into practice what they are learning.
- Allow her to share in the group, but at some point you will need closure if her emotions are strong. Simply say, "Let's take a minute and pray for Anne." Have a few share sentence prayers for her. Then go back to the discussion.

WOMEN NOT SHARING VULNERABLY OR HONESTLY
- Often the discussion leader needs to model this by sharing her own struggles with sin in group and in prayer.
- Ask a few of the more mature women, outside of group, to help you by paving the way and providing models.

WRONG ANSWERS
- A rebuke from the leader may cause a woman to drop out of the group. If you feel strongly about the danger of the answer, you can ask what someone else thinks, or suggest taking another look at the passage by going back to a "fact-gathering question."
- Trust the Spirit, for you do not need to do His job. He will guide the group into truth by having someone else speak up, prompting the woman to see her own error, and protecting the minds of the other women. Women are intuitive, and a simple "What does someone else think?" speaks volumes without crushing the woman who gave the wrong answer.

WEEK 1: A GLORIOUS BRIDE: EMBROIDERED WITH GOLD

We suggest highlighting the following questions for discussion. If time permits, answer others as well, but pace yourself to be sure to answer these. If you don't pace your group well, you should always skip to the last question. Many of the questions we skipped are "fact-gathering" questions, which, though essential to the application questions, don't lend themselves to discussion. However, if you find someone is off on her application, you may choose to go back to the "fact-gathering" question.

The "Getting Acquainted" Questions. Do both of them, but just hear from a few on question 2. Also, with question 1, tell them if nothing comes to their mind to feel free to tell the group their name and to say, "Pass."

Highlight these questions to discuss: 1, 2, 3 (just hear from a few), 6, 7, 8, 9, 15, 16, 19, 21, 24C, 26, 28

Day 1: Becoming His Betrothed

2. The confession is "Jesus is Lord." This is significant for those who try to separate Savior from Lord. When you trust Jesus, it must be for who He is. He is Lord. It is also vital to see that this must involve the heart, and not just the mouth. When you truly have received Jesus as your Lord in your heart, there will be a life change, for He has come to live in you. This is a genuine rather than a counterfeit salvation, and you will not be put to shame.

5. *Faithful.* If your conversion is genuine, there will be a desire to be faithful to the Lord, continuing in Him.

6. Both the wise and the foolish listened to Jesus' words. (Both were sitting in the pew at church!) Yet one obeyed because his conversion was genuine, and he desired to be faithful. The other did not obey, for it was just in his mouth, not in his heart.

7. If conversion is genuine, if God lives in you, then there *will* be a desire to be faithful. This does not mean you will not sin, but that the consistent direction of your life will be faithfulness to the Lord. The virgins who were not prepared never really knew the Lord, they only appeared to know the Lord. Therefore, Jesus said, "I never knew you," and the door was shut. When we die, there are no second chances.

Day 2: I Am Going Away to Prepare a Place for You

9. Many see this passage as a reference to heaven, and that Jesus has gone away to prepare a place for us.

10. Only the Father knows, and it will be unexpected, as was the Flood in the days of Noah. People will be going about life as usual, and suddenly one will be taken and one will be left. We need to be prepared. How do we do this? You can tell your group that the letter of John, which we will begin next week, will show us how we can become confident and unashamed at His coming.

    In the days of Jesus, it wasn't until the *father* said all was ready that the groom came back in a great processional with his friends, surprising the bride.

13. Faith or salvation—for the only thing that could cause us to be cast into hell is our rejection of Christ.

15. Women may feel that they are being prideful to share, but emphasize that the glory belongs to God. Explain that they are praising God by sharing specifics, and it will be an encouragement to other women who need to hear some victory stories! You may need to lead the way.

Day 3: We Ain't Going to Be the Same Woman

17. A. Light
    B. Truth
    C. Death *(If some said mercy, that is true as well.)*
    D. Mercy or love

Day 4: Thou Art the Fairest of Men

22. The anointing oil was so lavish on Jesus that when He comes from the beautiful place He has prepared for us (a palace adorned with ivory!) even His robes will be fragrant.

Day 5: A Glorious Bridegroom and a Beautiful Bride

24. B. The stars are visible in the most remote areas of the earth. Everyone can hear or see creation and know in his heart there must be a God. That is why every man is without excuse. If he truly acknowledges God, the implication is that God will reveal more to him.

25. A. An individual whose faith has been tested by the fires of life and found to be genuine.
    B. Faith proved genuine through trial.

26. Many answers are right. You might point out that we are told that faith comes through hearing the Word of God, so taking their homework seriously and always calling upon the Holy Spirit to reveal truth as they study will help their faith grow strong and genuine. It will sustain them through the fires of life.

Week 2: What Is She Wearing?

The "Icebreaker" Questions. Do both of them, but just hear from a few on each.

Highlight these questions to discuss: 1 (just have them call out a few of their answers), 5, 6, 7, 8, 10, 11, 12, 13, 14, 17, 20, 21

Day 1: The Imprint of a Christian

1. Don't feel like they must find them all—affirm them for any they have found—and if they are having trouble, direct them to a few of the following passages. They may find more, for there is repetition. They may be shocked at how black-and-white John's statements are. Let them know that will be addressed in Week 3.

Counterfeit	Genuine
Claims to walk in the light, but walks in darkness	(1:6–7) Walks in the light
Claims to be without sin	(1:8–9) Confesses sin
Claims to know Him but does not obey	(2:3–4) Obeys His commands
Claims to be in the light but hates his brother	(2:9–10) Loves his brother
Loves the world	(2:15) Does not love the world
Left the fellowship of believers	(2:19) Remained in the fellowship of believers
Denies that Jesus is the Christ	(2:22–23) Acknowledges the Son
Departs from what he heard in the beginning	(2:24–26) Remains in what he heard from the beginning and allows Spirit to teach him

Counterfeit	Genuine
Does have a life direction of sin	(3:7–10) Does not have a life direction in sin
Hates his brother	(1:14–15) Loves his brother
Has no mercy on his brother	(3:16–17) Lays down his life for his brother
Denies that Jesus came in the flesh	(4:2–3) Acknowledges that Jesus came in the flesh
Speaks from viewpoint of the world	(4:5–6) Does not speak from viewpoint of the world
Claims to love God but does not love brother	(4:7–8 and 4:20) Loves his brother
Does not believe in the Son of God	(5:10) Believes in the Son of God

DAY 2: COUNTERFEIT CLOTHES

2. B. If you truly love God and your neighbor, then you will obey all the rest. You will not worship other gods or take His name in vain. You will not murder or commit adultery, and so on.

4. B. He was trying to trap Jesus, because the Pharisees thought *He* had missed the most important things.

DAY 3: THE REAL DEAL

13. We can have genuine intimacy with the Lord. We can have a real depth of intimacy with other believers. Finally, though we will know sorrow, we can have a complete joy.

DAY 4: THE MOST IMPORTANT THING

17. Since our brother is our neighbor, in a sense, this is not a new commandment, but an old one. However, the Lord and John, as His messenger, have made this a new commandment in a sense by emphasizing the importance of loving our brother in particular.

DAY 5: A NEW COMMANDMENT

20. When a woman does her homework and memory work, she not only helps herself, she helps her sisters to grow in faith. Keeping confidences and really listening to one another are vital. A woman who talks easily might hold back, and the shy woman might trust God enough to share. Be sensitive to encourage one another through notes, hospitality, and kind words.

WEEK 3: BLACK AND WHITE

The "Icebreaker" Questions. Do both of them, but just hear from a few on each.

Highlight these questions to discuss: 3 (hear just a few), 5 (don't put anyone on the spot, but ask if anyone would be willing to share), 6, 7, 9, 10 (hear from a few), 11C, 12 (hear from a few), 13 (as many as want to share),14A, 17, 20, 21

Day 2: Dear Children, I Write These Things to You So You Will Not Sin

8. He is the only One without sin, so He can go to the Father. He is "the Righteous One."

9. If you give in to your sinful nature, you will die. This means they are heading back into bondage, back into chains. On the other hand, if they put to death the sinful nature, they are heading into true life, into freedom.

Day 5: Ancient of Foes

19. The anointing refers to the Holy Spirit, the third person of the Trinity, who can teach you and help you understand truths from the Word. It is vital that we remain in Him, that we abide, that we stay close, that we be still and ask Him to teach us.

20. A. If someone does not believe Jesus is who He claims to be—the Christ, the Lord—then that person is not a true believer. It is also a contradiction to say, "I believe in Jesus, but not God," or "I believe in God, but not Jesus." They are One.

    B. The persistent direction of a child of God is to do what is right. It does not mean he will not sin, but that the direction of his life is to do what is right. Jesus said we will be able to tell the counterfeit by their fruit, for a good tree does not bear bad fruit.

    C. We'll look at this more carefully later, but the ultimate lie is the one that does not confess Jesus is fully man and fully God. It preaches a different Jesus.

    D. Watch out if this person has the same viewpoint as the world and refuses to listen to believers.

Week 4: Walking in the Dark

The "Icebreaker" Questions. Do both of them, but just hear from a few on each. Be careful not to spend too much time on sibling rivalry stories.

Highlight these questions to discuss: 2 (all parts), 3, 5, 6, 7, 10, 13, 14, 15, 16 (don't put anyone on the spot, but ask if anyone would be willing to share), 18, 19 (all parts), 20, 21, 24, 27 (hear from one or two briefly), 31, 32, 33, and 35

Day 1: Darkness Is Our Natural State

1. B. When Isaiah truly saw God for who He was, in all His holiness, he was also able to see how he fell short, and so did all the people around him.

    C. The burning coal is like the cleansing fire of God. Isaiah had mentioned his "unclean lips." Now they are purified.

    D. Now, cleansed, he feels ready and eager to go: "Here am I. Send me!"

2. A. These were very experienced fishermen, and the advice of Jesus defied all the rules. So often that is the way with the Word of God—it is completely different from what makes sense to us.

    B. Like Isaiah, when he saw the power of Jesus, the wisdom of Jesus, he realized how terribly short he fell of the holiness of God.

    C. Point out that John was there—and John refers, in the opening of his letter, to actually seeing Jesus with his own eyes.

    D. It is when we realize our depravity and confess it that we are ready for service, ready to be fishers of men. David has a similar thought in Psalm 51:10–13.

3. You may need to lead the way in discussion by making yourself vulnerable.

DAY 2: DO NOT BE LIKE CAIN

10. Jesus lives in every believer, so when we bear malice toward a brother or sister, we are hating Jesus. Jesus asked Saul of Tarsus, "Why are you persecuting Me?"

12. B. It was the first of his flock, and it was the fat portions, which were considered the best of the animal.

DAY 3: FIRST CHANCE: CHOOSE TO STAY IN THE LIGHT

19. A. Even unbelievers have been given a conscience. God has put His law on our hearts. While our hearts can be seared, by persisting in the wrong, still, the voice of God is there.
    B. God's Word.
    C. The Holy Spirit will "remind" a believer of the Word of God, and illumine its meaning.

DAY 4: SECOND CHANCE: RESPOND TO THE CONVICTION OF GOD

30. The key to restoration is genuine repentance.

DAY 5: THIRD CHANCE: REPENT OF YOUR SIN

32. We should pray for our brothers. Overcoming sin is a fight, and we need to intercede for our brothers and sisters in Christ, that they will be strengthened to walk in the light, but that if they sin, their repentance will be genuine. Then, they will, as John promises, be forgiven and find life. That life is salvation for those who repent and come to Christ and ongoing life-giving strength for sins after conversion. We should not pray for the "counterfeit" brothers who reject Christ to be forgiven in another way. Of course, we can pray that they will come to Christ. This is a difficult passage, and there are other interpretations of it, but John Stott's makes the most sense to us. (See note in text.)

33. A. "Hands full of blood" refers to murder.
    B. "Crimson" is a picture of hands full of blood.

WEEK 5: WALKING IN THE LIGHT

The "Icebreaker" Questions. Do both of them, hearing from several.

Highlight these questions to discuss: 1, 2A, E, 4, 5A, B, F, 6 (all parts), 7, 8, 9, 10, 11, 12, 13, 16A, B, C, D, F, H, 17, 18, 19D, 20, 21B, C, D, 22B, D, 23, 26, 28, 29A, C, 30, 31

DAY 1: UNDERSTANDING AND OVERCOMING THE DECEIT OF OUR HEARTS

4. C. James mentions keeping a rein on our tongues, looking after orphans and widows in their distress, and keeping ourselves from being polluted by the world. John mentions doing what is right, not shutting up our compassions to those in need, not loving the world, and keeping ourselves from idols.

DAY 2: COUNTERFEIT # 1: EMOTIONAL REPENTANCE WITHOUT A U-TURN

5. C. After offering blind and lame sacrifices, after divorcing their wives, after withholding their tithes, they ask the Lord, "How have we defiled You?"

E. Because we have one Father, we are family. When we are unfaithful to one for whom Christ died, we are unfaithful to Him. Because believers are one with God, when we are unfaithful to another believer, we are unfaithful to God.

F. When we unite ourselves to an unbeliever, we defile God. (See 2 Corinthians 6:14–18.) God is also seeking godly offspring (Malachi 2:15) so He is grieved to have them exchange their Israelite wives for pagan women, as well as the primary grief over the treachery of casting out the wives of their covenant.

7. They have wearied God by justifying their behavior, calling evil good. Often believers will say that God led them to do something that is sinful, but John's letter emphasizes that God's Spirit and God's Word are never at odds. After calling evil good, the men of Malachi are miffed at God, saying, "Where is the God of justice?"

10. If you have someone in your group who has experienced divorce, you might ask her, privately and ahead of time, if she could share a few sentences about how believers might better minister to her.

12. "Revering God's name" means that you see Him as Lord and do what He commands. This is true repentance, and for those who repent He will bring healing and freedom.

DAY 3: COUNTERFEIT # 2: SORRY ABOUT THE CONSEQUENCES BUT NOT BROKEN BEFORE GOD

13. Saul may have been jealous of David's success with Goliath, of Jonathan's admiration for David, and it is clearly stated that he was jealous of the admiration the women had for David. His eyes were on the praise of men, not on pleasing God.

19. D. Had David been sorry for just the consequences, he might have grown bitter. But he knew he had sinned grievously, had wounded God, and deserved any consequences, even the death of his son.

DAY 5: PICK UP YOUR MAT AND WALK

28. C. You inspire others when you do your homework, your memory work, and are vulnerably honest about your struggles with sin. When you obey and experience victory, it encourages others that they can as well. When you show a heart of love by really listening to women and responding to their needs, they see Jesus in you.

WEEK 6: AUTUMN GLORY

The "Icebreaker" Questions. Do both of them, hearing from several.

Highlight these questions to discuss: 1, 4A, B, C, 5, 8, 9D, E, F (F is optional for sharing), 10, 11, 12, 13, 15A, B, 16, 17, 18A, B, D, H, 19, 20, 21, 22, 23B, 25 (have a few share one), 26 (as many as time permits)

DAY 1: DO NOT LOVE THE WORLD

4. A. Food is a gift; gluttony is harmful. It makes you tired to overeat, as does carrying extra weight. Marital sex is a gift, but outside marriage it becomes destructive—it hurts you emotionally, spiritually, and physically. Inflamed lusts sap your strength.

B. It takes time and money to think about and care for material things. These cannot last, so it is "vanity," which means something passing swiftly away.

Day 3: Overcoming the Lust of the Flesh

9. D. Joseph did not want to sin against God. If we are refraining from only sin to avoid the consequences, then when we think we can avoid the consequences, there is nothing to refrain us. But one consequence we will *always* have is that we will leave the presence and power of God. Repeatedly, we are told God was *with* Joseph. Joseph did not want to leave the presence of God.

   E. Day after day he refused her. Finally, he fled.

   F. Don't put anyone on the spot, but if someone is willing to share her plan or something she has done that has led to victory, ask her to share.

15. A. James says friendship with the world is hatred toward God. John says that if you love the world, the love of God is not in you. You cannot love both—Jesus says you cannot have two masters. Remember that loving the world means embracing its values. You cannot, for example, both love God and love sexual immorality. You must choose your Master.

Day 4: Overcoming the Lust of the Eyes

18. I. Abraham actually expected God to raise Isaac from the dead after he had sacrificed him.

20. V. 5: In the midst of this enormous test, Abraham believed God was worthy of worship; v. 8: "God himself will provide"; v. 14: "The Lord will provide."

Give a special encouragement to the women to get started on their homework early this next week. They will be delving into Esther. It's fascinating, but in order to participate intelligently in the discussion next week, they will need to have done their homework.

Week 7: It's Not Easy Being Green

The "Icebreaker" Questions. Do all of them, hearing from several.

Highlight these questions to discuss: 1B, D, F, G, I; 2; 3A, B, 5 (all parts), 6 (all parts), 7, 9B, D, 10 (only if someone wants to share) 12, 15A, C, F, 16 (only if someone wants to share), 18, 19, 20, 21, 22

Day 1: It's Not Easy Being Queen

1. G. The pride of Xerxes and Haman is almost unbelievable, as illustrated by verses like Esther 1:4. Continually, they seem like hot-air balloons, only to be deflated by a pinprick from God, as happened to Xerxes in this chapter when Vashti refused to come. This is a pattern in Esther. In contrast, Esther and Mordecai are elevated after they humble themselves and step out in faith. It is a story exemplifying how God exalts the humble and brings down the proud. Help the women look for and enjoy the humor.

   I. One year of beauty treatments and five years between becoming queen and the edict for the holocaust add up to six years. The unknown factor is how long it was between the end of the beauty treatments and the winning of the contest. Some historians think the war against Greece occurred during this time—and that it was a four-year war. It's difficult to know, but we do know that Esther hid her faith for a long time.

J. When you look at this verse along with Esther 2:7, there seems to be evidence of love and concern on Mordecai's part. Some commentators believe that Mordecai was politically ambitious and entered Esther because he thought she would win. Though that is possible, the phrases "many girls were brought" and "Esther also was taken" (Esther 2:8) connote that Mordecai did not "enter" her but that she was taken.

DAY 2: THE CONTROVERSY IN THE BOOK OF ESTHER

5. B. The women may not be familiar with the decadence in the book of Judges. There is raging lust, deceit, and a terrible abuse of women. The story in Judges 19 is so awful it is difficult to read. So it is significant that the book of Judges ends with this verse, showing how decadent we can become without the light of God. Our hearts truly are deceitful, as Jeremiah says, and if we live by what is right in our own eyes, we will sink to this decadence. This truth has been exemplified again and again in history. So as soon as we are measuring behavior on the basis of "what makes sense" instead of God's Word, we are measuring with a faulty ruler.

   C. It is a common error in judgment to think that prosperity is evidence of God's pleasure in an individual. God's time scale is different from ours, and He may be withholding judgment temporarily. This is why Proverbs warns us again and again not to envy the prosperity of the wicked.

   D. Our deceitful hearts lead us to believe that God may be leading us to have an abortion or to marry an unbeliever, but God cannot go against His character or His Word. We are building on the sand when we do this rather than on the solid rock. The discussion may lead into situations such as smuggling Bibles into closed countries or hiding Jews during Word War II. We believe that the difference in these situations is that the motivation is love. Some may say this was true of Esther as well, but Mordecai and Esther did not know that a holocaust was to follow. It seemed that fear, rather than love, was their motivation.

   F. "Blameless" does not mean sinless, but living in continual repentance. The only way we can know when we have moved into the shadows is to measure ourselves in the searching light of God's Spirit and God's Word. This same psalm says, "Your word is a lamp to my feet and a light for my path" (Psalm 119:105).

6. Have them correlate verses with these questions. There are verses in their last question that provide light, but they may think of others. A. Proverbs 3:5 and 12:3; B. Luke 12:4–5; C. Ecclesiastes 8:11; D. Psalm 119:1 and Isaiah 61:3.

7. We have often failed miserably as a body of believers in showing compassion to the woman who chooses abortion or the individual in a homosexual lifestyle. Calling them names only hardens their hearts toward God. Showing them love may help them to be willing to walk toward the light. Sometimes we fear that coming close is an endorsement, but it is not. That was the mistake the Pharisees made. They condemned Jesus for eating with sinners, not realizing that He was loving them into the light. It is completely possible to love someone and yet not condone their sin. You might ask them how the family that loved Andrea, in the last lesson, exemplified this.

Day 3: The Sins of Our Fathers and the Grace of God

9. B. All of these believers were willing to face death rather than go against God. They thought God *would* deliver them, but even if He did not, they would not do wrong. It is interesting that later, Esther's response in Esther 4:16 is similar to the three young men's response in Daniel 3:17–18. It is also interesting to note that these three young men had each other, but until Esther 4, Esther was alone. It is only in Esther 4, after Mordecai has repented, that she has *his* support. It is often hard to walk the narrow road alone. We need strong believers in our lives.

12. God is compassionate toward His children. When they are being abused, as we believe Esther was, He does not turn away. When they make poor choices, as we believe Mordecai and even Esther (in obeying Mordecai in this instance) did, God is compassionate. If you have been abused, God saw, and it broke His heart. He can bring beauty out of the ashes. If you have made poor choices, God still loves you and still extends His hand to you.

Week 8: True Blue

The "Icebreaker" Questions. Do both of them, but just hear from a few on each. *Highlight these questions to discuss. Pace yourself to make sure you get to the vital questions in Days 4 and 5. The opening days should go quite quickly. Answer questions 2, 3, 4, 5, 6, 7, 9, 10, 11, 13, 14, 15, 19A, E, and F; 21, 22, 23, 24, 26, 27, 28, 29, 31, 34, 35*

Day 1: You Are Who You Are Around

4. Many churches and even whole denominations who were once healthy are no longer healthy. Being centered on the Word of God is vital to health, but how can you tell if a church really is? If the Word is truly being preached from the pulpit with the power of the Holy Spirit, and the people are walking in that truth, you should see the principles of 1 John being lived out. The people should have a desire to walk in the light; there should be real love and an absence of division. People should be living sacrificially, and that will be seen in giving, in missions, in a spirit of humble service. Every church will fall short of God's holiness, but a healthy church realizes these things and the people are living in genuine repentance.

5. Most interpret the anointing of the Holy One to be the Holy Spirit. The words of Jesus in John's Gospel are very similar when He talks about the Holy Spirit, who will teach and remind them of what they learned from the beginning. (See John 14:25–26.)

6. The Holy Spirit can never lie. The Holy Spirit can make it possible for believers to understand the Word of God, even without a teacher. This does not mean teachers are not valuable, but that God has sent the ultimate Teacher to live within us.

9. When they give an example, ask them to support it with Scripture. For example, we know that God's Spirit does not lead us to speak disrespectfully to our parents because His Word says: "Honor your father and mother" (Ephesians 6:2).

Day 3: It Speaks from the Viewpoint of the World

14. *Who is John talking about? Where are they from? What characterizes them?*

v. 4 believers ("children")	God	overcome false spirits

| v. 5 unbelievers | the world | speak as the world and the world listens |
| v. 6 believers | God | believers listen and the world does not |

15. The false spirit has the same perspective as those apart from God—and those people listen and agree. The true Spirit has a different perspective, and the world doesn't listen.

16. A. (Lust of Flesh) Esther 1:10–11; 2:2–4; 2:12–14
    B. (Lust of Eyes) Esther 1:4–7
    C. (Pride of Life) Esther 1:4; 1:12; Esther 1:12–21

DAY 4: TRUE BLUE

29. She is coming out of the shadows and telling the truth about her identity; she is willing to lay down her life; and she is showing mercy toward her brothers and sisters.

DAY 5: GOD ON THE MOVE

31. Most believe Esther was doing this in obedience to the wisdom God had given her. However, because there is no editorial comment, we can only speculate. Some believe she was overcome with fear and was procrastinating; however, even if that is true, God still worked in that, giving time for the heart of the king to be softened.

WEEK 9: WHITE AS SNOW

Hear from as many as wish to share in the "Icebreaker" questions. You may want to go around giving women the choice of answering either one. *Highlight these questions to discuss: 3, 6, 7, 8A and B, 10, 12, 13, 14, 15, 16, 17, 19, 22, 24, 25 (all parts), 26*

DAY 1: GOD IS MERCY, SO WE MUST BE MERCIFUL

1. C. Grief (for the brokenhearted) Luke 15:20 (he was watching and waiting—*filled* with compassion); Luke 15:24 and 32 (understood pain of being lost and "dead"); Luke 15:28 (went out to older son, grieved over his pain)
    Forgiveness (for the transgressor): Luke 15:20 (immediate, didn't hold back); Luke 15:28 (again, immediate response to older son)
    Generosity (for those in need): Luke 15:22–23 (everything was the best); Luke 15:31 (all that he has is his)

DAY 2: GRIEF FOR THE BROKENHEARTED

5. The Bible speaks frequently of the Lord's compassion. It was not nails that held our Savior to the cross, but love and compassion.

8. A. Esther 4:15–16
    What she did: fasted (and we assume prayed) and asked others to join her
    Principle: seek God's wisdom and favor before you plan or act
    B. Esther 7:3–4
    What she did: She had listened carefully to God and now to Xerxes and heard him offer her a "petition" and a "request," so she seized the chance to ask for two favors.
    Principle: Be still before God before you move. Approach people with great diplomacy.

Listen to them carefully and respond to their words so that they know you have listened to them.

Day 3: Forgiveness for the Transgressor

12. We have been forgiven so much. How can we not forgive?

13. The younger son was ungrateful and disrespectful to ask for his inheritance early. Then he wasted it on sinful pleasures, though the father may have worked hard for this money. The older son was ungrateful and lacking in compassion for his own brother.

14. Don't put anyone on the spot, but this could lead to good sharing. Consider making yourself vulnerable.

15. Don't put anyone on the spot, but this could lead to good sharing.

18. We are *always* called to forgive. However, if the transgressor has not shown genuine repentance, there is no sin in drawing boundaries to protect yourself. David forgave Saul from his heart, but he fled when it became evident Saul's repentance was counterfeit. God gives provision, for example, for a woman to separate from her abusive husband. You do not need to trust someone who has not repented, but you do, with the help of God, need to have compassion for him in his spiritual darkness and to forgive him.

Day 5: May I Be His Love to You

24. A. That he is born of God and knows God. We are totally depraved. Anything good in us is from God.

    B. If you don't love, you don't know God. (Remember, John is talking about the persistent direction of your life—for true believers will fail.)

    D. Make sure they don't miss this: As we love one another, we manifest Christ to one another. We make the invisible Lord visible!

    G. John is reviewing the importance of understanding the true identity of Christ. Here he emphasizes His humanity, but it is also important to remember His deity. Understanding and receiving the true Jesus is the key to being a Christian. We also manifest Him by relying on His love and allowing His love to flow to others.

Week 10: Clothed in the Many-Splendored Colors of His Love

We recommend dividing this lesson into two weeks for discussion so that you can answer all the questions together. If you are able to do this, assign the first two days as homework for the first week and the last three as homework for the second week. *If you are unable to do this, highlight the following questions: 4 (all parts), 5 (all parts), 6, 7, 9, 10, 11, 13, 14, 15, 16, 17, 19, 21, 28, 31, 40, 44*

Day 1: What Is She Wearing?

1. The Samaritan was doing a better job of bearing the mark of a Christian (love).

2. Religion rather than relationship. Outward appearance instead of the heart. Because our nature is depraved, we do the same. How we need to rely on the grace and love of God!

3. A. Important things are said when time is running out.

7. It represents salvation, but if that salvation is genuine, there will be righteous acts.

8. If God truly lives within us, He will be transforming us, and when we see Him, He will make us pure. If God truly lives within us, we will want to persist in purity. The five virgins who were not ready did not truly have Him living inside them.

9. Light: God is Light (1 John 1:5).
   Death: Jesus laid down His life (1 John 3:16).
   Truth: The Holy Spirit cannot lie (1 John 2:27).
   Mercy: God is Love (1 John 4:8).

Day 2: Clothed in Light

17. Weeping and wailing at the altar, yet they had still abandoned their wives. There was no change in behavior.

21. The grace that forgave you continues in you. The faithfulness you saw in the beginning continues. The Word you knew in the beginning continues to be a resource for you.

Day 3: Clothed in Death

26. Xerxes' decadent party seemed motivated by pride, and it brought great harm to his wife and to the women of Persia. Mordecai and Haman were continuing an ancient feud motivated by pride.

Day 4: Clothed in Truth

35. Xerxes was very quick to listen to the bad advice and the lies brought to him from people in the world.

37. You will die as well. God will use someone else somewhere else. This may very well be God's calling for you right now.

Day 5: Clothed in Mercy

42. We will have greater confidence that we belong to the truth, even if we tend to have a condemning heart. If we are doing these things and our heart continues to condemn us, we must trust God, who is greater than our hearts. We can have confidence that God hears our prayers.

43. As we live out these principles, we become like Jesus in the world, and we can actually tangibly love Jesus and be loved by Jesus through the body of Christ. John had promised that we could know the same kind of intimacy that he knew with Jesus, and this is the fulfillment, in part, of that promise.

APPENDIX B: SONGS

CHORUS OF "MAY I BE HIS LOVE TO YOU"

May I be His love to you
May I lift your eyes toward heaven
May I come to you and lead you to His light
May I cry His tears for you
May I be the place that you can run to
Where you'll hear His voice
And see Him in my eyes
All your life may I be His love

1 JOHN SONGS

"This Is My Commandment"

This is my commandment that you love one another
That your joy may be full
This is my commandment that you love one another
That your joy may be full

That your joy may be full
That your joy may be full
This is my commandment that you love one another
That your joy may be full

"Beloved, Let Us Love One Another"

Beloved, let us love one another,
for love is of God, and everyone who loveth
is born of God, and knoweth God.
He that loveth not,
knoweth not God, for God is love.

Beloved, let us love one another.
First John, four, seven and eight.

"Greater Is He That Is in Me"

Greater is He that is in me
Greater is He that is in me
Greater is He that is in me
Than he that is in the world

PRAISE CHORUSES

"Be Glorified"

In my life, Lord, be glorified, be glorified
In my life, Lord, be glorified today.

In your Bride, Lord, be glorified, be glorified
In your Bride, Lord, be glorified today.

"Seek Ye First"

Seek ye first the Kingdom of God
and His righteousness
and all these things will be added unto you
Allelu, Alleluia.

HYMNS

"Fairest Lord Jesus"

Fairest Lord Jesus, ruler of all nature,
O thou of God and man the Son, thee will I cherish,
Thee will I honor, thou, my soul's glory, joy and crown!

Fair are the meadows, fairer still the woodlands,
Robed in the blooming garb of spring: Jesus is fairer,
Jesus is purer, who makes the woeful heart to sing.

Fair is the sunshine, fairer still the moonlight,

And all the twinkling starry host: Jesus shines brighter,
Jesus shines purer, than all the angels heaven can boast.

Beautiful Savior! Lord of all nations!
Son of God and Son of Man! Glory and honor,
Praise, adoration, now and forevermore be thine!
(Public Domain)

"The Battle Hymn of the Republic"

Mine eyes have seen the glory of the coming of the Lord;
He is trampling out the vintage where the grapes of wrath are stored;
He hath loosed the fateful lightning of His terrible swift sword;
His truth is marching on.

Glory! Glory! Hallelujah! Glory! Glory! Hallelujah! Glory! Glory! Hallelujah!
His truth is marching on.

He has sounded forth the trumpet that shall never sound retreat;
He is sifting out the hearts of men before His judgment seat.
Oh, be swift, my soul, to answer Him; be jubilant, my feet;
Our God is marching on.

Glory! Glory! Hallelujah! Glory! Glory! Hallelujah! Glory! Glory! Hallelujah!
Our God is marching on.
(Public Domain)

"Grace Greater Than Our Sin"

Grace, grace, God's grace
Grace that will pardon and cleanse within;
Grace, grace, God's grace
Grace that is greater than all our sin!
(Public Domain)

"Breathe on Me, Breath of God"

Breathe on me, Breath of God, fill me with life anew
That I may love what Thou dost love and do what Thou wouldst do

Breathe on me, Breath of God, till I am wholly Thine,
Till all this earthly part of me glows with Thy fire divine.
(Public Domain)

"What Can Wash Away My Sin?"

What can wash away my sin?
Nothing but the blood of Jesus;

What can make me whole again?
Nothing but the blood of Jesus.

O precious is the flow
That makes me white as snow;
No other fount I know,
Nothing but the blood of Jesus.
(Public Domain)

Appendix C: Movie Night

Tri-Mark's *Esther*

Make it a fun night with popcorn. Afterward, give whoever desires the opportunity to answer the following questions. This movie can be rented in Christian bookstores or purchased from Christianbook.com or deebrestin.com.

1. What stood out to you from this presentation of *Esther*?

2. Explain if you agreed or disagreed with the way the following people were portrayed:

   Xerxes or Ahasuerus
   Mordecai
   Esther
   Haman

3. Did the movie give you any additional insight into Esther? If so, what?

4. Where did you see the movie being true to Scripture? Untrue?

5. What do you think has most impacted you in your walk with God from the story of Esther?

Appendix D: Resources

deebrestin.com

Find out where Dee is speaking, write to her, discover her book and movie recommendations, and take advantage of sales when you order books, videos, and study guides on-line.

troccoli.com

Find out where Kathy is speaking and singing, sign up for her Candle Club, and order her books and CDs.

Further Study on 1 John or Esther

You have just completed a topical study of 1 John and Esther. Dee has also written book studies:

> *A Woman's Journey Through Esther*
> *A Woman of Joy (1 John)*

These are available through deebrestin.com or Christianbook.com or at your local Christian bookstore.

For those struggling with homosexuality or with a loved one involved in homosexuality:

Andrea or Richard Yates
P.O. Box 11469
Philadelphia, PA 19111
Rich: rich@harvestusa.org (Phone: 215-342-7114)
Andrea: stopthecycle@juno.com

Recommendations for Giving

We recommend that you choose ministries approved by the
Evangelical Council for Financial Accountability
440 W. Jubal Early Drive, Suite 130
Winchester, VA 22601
1-800-323-9473

We recommend all of the following ministries.
Learn more about them through their Web sites.

Far East Broadcasting Company
P.O. Box 1
La Mirada, CA 90637-0001
www.febc.org
febc@febc.org

International Students, Inc.
P.O. Box C
Colorado Springs, CO 80901
1-800-ISI-TEAM
www.isionline.org
information@isionline.org

MAP International
2200 Glynco Parkway
Brunswick, GA 31525-6800
www.map.org
map@map.org

World Concern
19303 Fremont Avenue North
Seattle, WA 98133
1-800-755-5022
www.worldconcern.org
info@worldconcern.org

World Vision
P.O. Box 9716
Federal Way, WA 98063-9716
1-888-511-6598
www.worldvision.org

Notes

Week 1: A Glorious Bride: Embroidered with Gold

1. John Calvin, *Calvin's Commentaries, Volume XVII, Harmony of the Evangelists, Volume 3* (Grand Rapids: Baker Books, 1999), 170.

2. Max Lucado, *When Christ Comes* (Nashville: Word Publishing, 1999), 8.

3. John Calvin, *Calvin's Commentaries, Volume XVI* (Grand Rapids: Baker Books, 1999), 174.

4. Charles Binnie, quoted in *The Treasury of David, Volume 1* (Peabody: Hendrickson Publishers, 1876), 323.

5. Jonathan Edwards, quoted in *The Treasury of David, Volume 1* (Peabody: Hendrickson Publishers, 1876), 282.

6. Charles Spurgeon, *The Treasury of David, Volume 1* (Peabody: Hendrickson Publishers, 1876), 320–21.

7. Lucado, *When Christ Comes*, 145.

Week 2: What Is She Wearing?

1. Kathy Troccoli, *My Life Is in Your Hands* (Grand Rapids: Zondervan Publishing House, 1997), 75.

2. Francis A. Schaeffer, *The Mark of a Christian* (Downers Grove: InterVarsity, 1971), 16.

3. Ibid., 22–23.

4. Ibid., 8–13.

Week 3: Black and White

1. Charles Spurgeon, *The Comprehensive Spurgeon Collection* [CD-ROM] (Ages Software, 2001), first sermon on John 2:12.

2. John R.W. Stott, *The Letters of John* (Grand Rapids: Eerdmans, 2000), 99.

Week 4: Walking in the Dark

1. John R.W. Stott, *The Epistles of John* (Grand Rapids: Eerdmans, 1983), 141.

2. Spurgeon, *The Comprehensive Spurgeon Collection*.

3. Dallas Willard, *The Divine Conspiracy* (San Francisco: HarperCollins, 1998), 1.

4. Schaeffer, *The Mark of a Christian*, 22–23.

WEEK 5: WALKING IN THE LIGHT

1. M. R. DeHaan, *Dear Doctor: I Have a Question . . .* (Grand Rapids: Zondervan, 1961), 169–70.

2. Oswald Chambers, *My Utmost for His Highest, An Updated Edition in Today's Language,* ed. James Reiman (Grand Rapids: Discovery House, 1992), Nov. 19.

3. Darrell L. Bock, *The Bible Knowledge Key Word Study, The Gospels* (Colorado Springs: Cook Communications, 2002), 291.

WEEK 6: AUTUMN GLORY

1. John Piper, *Desiring God, Revised Edition* (Sisters, Oreg.: Multnomah Books, 1996), 284.

2. Charles Spurgeon, *The Comprehensive Spurgeon Collection* [CD-ROM] (Ages Software, 2001), "Joseph Attacked by the Archers, no. 17," a sermon delivered on Sabbath morning, April 1, 1855.

3. Bock, *The Bible Knowledge Key Word Study,* 222.

WEEK 7: IT'S NOT EASY BEING GREEN

1. Herodotus, *Histories* (New York: Penguin, 1996), 459.

2. Flavius Josephus, "The Antiquities of the Jews," *Josephus: Complete Works,* trans. by William Whiston (Grand Rapids: Kregel Publications, 1981), 237.

3. Ibid., 35.

4. Joyce Baldwin, *Esther, Tyndale Old Testament Commentaries, Vol. 3* (Wheaton: Tyndale, 1984), 66.

5. Ibid., 48.

6. F. B. Huey, *The Expositor's Commentary, Vol. 4,* ed. Frank E. Gaebelein and Richard P. Polcyn (Grand Rapids: Zondervan, 1988), 793.

7. John MacArthur, *The MacArthur Study Bible* (Nashville: W Publishing Group, 1997), 682.

8. R. C. Sproul, editor, *The Reformation Study Bible* (Nashville: Thomas Nelson, 1995), 18.

9. John F. Brug, *People's Commentary Bible, Ezra-Nehemiah-Esther* (St. Louis: Concordia, 1985), 155–56.

10. Frederic Bush, *Word Biblical Commentary, Vol. 9* (Dallas: Word Books, 1996), 385.

11. John C. Whitcomb, *Esther: Triumph of God's Sovereignty* (Chicago: Moody, 1979), 66.

WEEK 8: CLOTHED IN TRUTH

1. Stott, *The Epistles of John,* 141.

2. Stephen S. Smalley, *Word Biblical Commentary, Vol. 51* (Dallas: Word Books, 1984), 105.

WEEK 9: CLOTHED IN MERCY

1. Max Lucado, *When Christ Comes* (Nashville: Word Publishing, 1999), p. xv, xvi.

2. Henri Nouwen, *The Return of the Prodigal* (New York: Doubleday, 1994), 4.

3. Ibid., 122.

4. Joyce Baldwin, *Esther, Tyndale Old Testament Commentary* (Downers Grove: Inter-Varsity, 1978), 95.

5. Ellie Lofaro, *Slices of Life: Unexpected Blessings from Real Relationships* (Colorado Springs, Colorado: David C. Cook Publishing Co., 2002), 13.

6. Stott, *The Epistles of John,* 190.

7. John F. Walyoord & Roy B. Zuck, *The Bible Knowledge Commentary, New Testament Edition* (Wheaton, Ill.: Victor Books, 1983), 899.

WEEK 10: CLOTHED IN THE MANY-SPLENDORED COLORS OF HIS LOVE

1. James C. Humes and Richard M. Nixon, *The Wit and Wisdom of Winston Churchill: A Treasury of More Than 1,000 Quotations and Anecdotes* (New York: HarperPerennial, 1995), 215.

2. Stott, *The Epistles of John,* 141.

ACKNOWLEDGMENTS

We (Dee and Kathy) would especially like to thank individuals from W Publishing Group, particularly Mark Sweeney, Ami McConnell, and Debbie Wickwire.

How thankful we are for a talented and caring editor in Wendy Wood. Wendy, despite enormous pressure in your personal life, you carried this off like the professional you are.

Thanks to the production staff at Thomas Nelson for their work on an amazingly creative video: Harry Clayton—thank you for choosing Russ Hall, one of the most talented men we have ever known to do this video. Russ, we will never forget the sacrifices you and your partners made to make this video the best. A special thanks to Jeff Hockman and Graham Bustin.

Dee's staff has been wonderful. Her new manager, Jill Johnson, has been incredible. Thanks also to Mary Jo Chatelain and Nanette Branch for all their valuable work. Thanks to Matt Baugher for his invaluable input at the videotaping and for acquiring permissions to use songs.

Thank you to Dee's mother, for allowing the photograph of her as a bride, and to Susan Stewart, for her photograph of Kathy as "a bride." And thank you, again, to Bart Larson for generously allowing us to use his photograph of autumn leaves. Please check Bart's Web site at www.reflectionsofglory.com.

And how can we thank our prayer teams, friends, and families enough for interceding so faithfully for us? Dee would particularly like to thank her husband, Steve, who is a servant-leader of great integrity, and also her church, Trinity Presbyterian, for their enormous support in hosting our practice session, praying for us, and loving us with the love of Jesus. There are those individuals across this nation who faithfully pray for our walk and for the anointing and wisdom of God for us. You receive little credit from man, but we pray the prayer of Boaz for you:

May the LORD repay you for what you have done. May you be richly rewarded by the LORD, the God of Israel, under whose wings you have come to take refuge. (Ruth 2:12)